9/10/99

To Ken & Maddi

I enjoyed your "A ...
presentation. I felt ...
the importance of our work.

with many Blessings,

Ken S...

9-10-99

Dear Ken,

I also enjoyed being a part
of your audience. I wish you
well with your new book.

Warm Regards,

Tom Knoblauch

Ken Lakritz (707) 253-5309

Thomas M. Knoblauch
1177 Willow Ave
Napa, CA. 94559
(707) 253-1218

Elders on
LOVE

ELDERS ON LOVE

Dialogues on the Consciousness, Cultivation, and Expression of Love

KENNETH R. LAKRITZ, PH.D. &

THOMAS M. KNOBLAUCH, PH.D.

Foreword by Rabbi Zalman M. Schachter-Shalomi,
Coauthor of *From Age-ing to Sage-ing*®

PARABOLA BOOKS
NEW YORK

Photographs by Jennifer Leigh Sauer

Library of Congress Cataloging-in-Publication Data
Lakritz, Kenneth R. (Kenneth Robert), 1958-
  Elders on love : dialogues on the consciousness, cultivation, and expression of love / Kenneth R. Lakritz & Thomas M. Knoblauch ; foreword by Zalman M. Schachter-Shalomi.
     p. cm.
  Includes bibliographical references.
  ISBN 0-930407-41-5 (alk. paper). — ISBN 0-930407-45-8 (pbk. : alk. paper)
     1. Aged—Psychology. 2. Aged—Interviews. 3. Love.
  I. Knoblauch, Thomas M. (Thomas Morrison), 1951- . II. Title.
  BF724.8L42 1999
  155.67'18—dc21   98-44297
                                                       CIP

Published by the Society for the Study of Myth and Tradition
656 Broadway, New York, NY 10012

06 05 04 03 02 01 00 99
10 9 8 7 6 5 4 3 2 1

The authors and publisher gratefully acknowledge permission to reprint the following material:

"A heartbreak shakes the yellow leaves..." by Rumi, from *The Return of the Mother* by Andrew Harvey. North Atlantic Books, 1995. Reprinted by permission of Balthazar Productions.

"Don't Go Back to Sleep" by Rumi, from *The Essential Rumi,* translated by Coleman Barks. Originally published by Threshold Books, 139 Main Street, Brattleboro, Vermont 05301.

"The freedom that is our nature..." by Thomas Merton, from *The Thomas Merton Reader* (New York: Image Books, 1996). Copyright © 1974 by the Merton Legacy Trust. Reprinted with permission.

"The Holy Longing" by Johann Wolfgang von Goethe, from *News of the Universe* by Robert Bly. Reprinted by permission of Sierra Club Books, San Francisco, California.

"On Love" and "On Marriage" from *The Prophet* by Kahlil Gibran. Copyright © 1923 by Kahlil Gibran and renewed 1951 by Administrators CTA of Kahlil Gibran Estate and Mary G. Gibran. Reprinted by permission of Alfred A. Knopf, Inc.

"One, One, One" from *Light upon Light: Inspirations from Rumi* by Andrew Harvey. Copyright © 1996 by Andrew Harvey. Used by arrangement with North Atlantic Books, Berkeley, California.

"A Ritual to Read to Each Other" by William Stafford. Copyright © 1998 by the Estate of William Stafford. Reprinted from *The Way It Is: New & Selected Poems by William Stafford* with the permission of Graywolf Press, Saint Paul, Minnesota.

In memory of Ken's father,

Arnold Herbert Lakritz (1929–1998),

A wise elder, a seeker of deeper truth,

and an example of love.

CONTENTS

The wise are wise only because they love.

—PAULO COELHO

My life is my message.

—MAHATMA GANDHI

FOREWORD

IN MEMORY OF
Victor Frankl

VICTOR FRANKL brought us the realization that what keeps us alive isn't happiness but meaning. It buys us life space—to use Kurt Lewin's expression. We wouldn't have space for an inner life if we didn't have meaning. Frankl describes how, in concentration camps, there were some who had given up on life and lost their life space and meaning. The will to live becomes extinguished in people who no longer have either a love or a meaning to hold onto.

This happens also to the aged. Victor Frankl shares with us that after you grow out of the issues of libido and the issues of power (so you are done with the Freud stuff and with the Adler stuff), you get a little bit more into the young creative artist of Rank and then Jung and the archetypal great visions. But, when you get somewhat older, you see that what keeps you going every day is the fact that you have covenants of love and meaning with other people—and that you are looking forward to the next stage of life to be able to fulfill your part in these covenants.

Much of the thinking of gerontology has to do with custodial care—or, as some would say more graphically, warehousing the redundant population until they are removed from the scene. We want to bring a different sense to it for a very selfish reason. We have lived through the sixties and seventies and have seen the possibilities of becoming sensitized and having our consciousness expanded. If we start thinking of how we would want to spend our last years, and we look around at what's mostly available today, we just don't want that. A lot of people would choose a deliberate exit rather than to be "warehoused."

On the other hand, we also have the dream that our harvest years might be employed for better things, the first of which is to use the extended life span for transforming oneself from being merely old into becoming an elder. I call this the October work. This involves life review and re-contextualizing experiences from the past.

Then, there opens up an area of pressing need for the planet. Earth (Gaia) desperately needs elders to serve her toward healing, and this is what she is hothousing us for. Service is the November work. I think that, instead of sending young people at the beginning of their lives to hot spots, we need to send an elder corps to Bosnia. After all, what have they got to lose? In this way elders could repay the planet for the goodness of life. Imagine us doing reconciliation work and saying to the grandparents on both sides of a conflict, "Let's sit down. Doesn't it hurt?"

Turning to a Bosnian, I can say, "I grieve with you for the grandchildren you lost," and turning to a Serb I can say, "I grieve with you for the grandchildren you lost. Is there a way in which we can make some sense out of that?" So we bring elder-mind into this situation or elder-mind into board rooms where, instead of thinking of the quarterly bottom line, we start thinking in terms of seven generations and all the things that we are now desperately trying to heal (because we acted without elder minds). And, clearly, Earth needs elder minds. Jimmy and Rosalynn Carter are wonderful examples of November work—people who act out of love and meaning.

Next there is the December work, which is to make the transition not tragic and desperate, but a good completion, like at the end of a symphony where you bring the themes of love and life into a reprise, encapsulating the whole experience into a symphony. Ending life in such a way gives meaning for people. Some, very deeply religious and spiritual, may say, "When my time comes I want to dissolve in the infinite ocean." Or for another person it might be, "I want to just fly to the heart of God." Someone else might express such sentiments as, "What a wonderful experience to live on earth! Other molecules never had that kind of experience."

So all these things have to do with changing the template of what it means to age. And here is where this book by Ken Lakritz and Tom Knoblauch is so important, because it brings examples from people who, as they describe their loving and their connection, have poured out their soul in their meaning-giving to life.

The issues of libido are not the same when a person gets older, because there isn't so much the urge to transmit to the next generation the genetic information of one organism, but rather there's the desire to take the cultural and civilizational information and pass it on. So elder people are still in a way making love, but this is not a physically erotic affair but an intergenerational thing. It is making love to the planet by wanting to "upload" experience and meaning into the working memory, if you will, of the planetary computer. Instead of focusing the love into this particular organism and body with whom I wanted to beget the next generation, as I did in my youth, I am now much more interested in relating to and loving and healing the planet. With the concern that I have for my grandchildren, and as I get in touch with how much I care for them, I shudder to think what kind of a world I am leaving them. Because of this, the need to change the template of what it means to age in society has become very pressing. Elders need social security, and I am not referring to finances alone but to social esteem and dignity. And furthermore—why cannot elders fall in love again and experience romance and eros?

In this book, as you read about these elders' experiences, you see not only how the template is shifting as far as the concepts are concerned, but how the affective life is being transformed. New models and ideals present themselves to readers of this book. My reading of it helped me crystallize again the way in which I would like my elder years to be of a quality that I call noble. And this nobility shows throughout all the pages of these interviews as these elders talk about significance and meaning. Aging will no longer remain as something where redundant population is warehoused, but, on the contrary, it will be a way in which a person can complete the life harvest and thank Earth.

This view of aging also takes the sting out of dying. I no longer see death as a dire emergency that has to be fought with all measures, but more as a crowning achievement, a sacred conclusion. Psychologists and others, including Carl Jung, have often talked about the phenomenon of closure. And once I see how other people such as these elders are coming to terms with aging and closure, I see something heroic and wonderful in it. So many thanks to you, Ken Lakritz and Tom Knoblauch, for gathering and presenting these words of elder-wisdom to the world!

RABBI ZALMAN M. SCHACHTER-SHALOMI
Co-author of *From Age-ing to Sage-ing®*
President, Spiritual Eldering Institute
World Wisdom Chair, Naropa Institute

PREFACE

If you bring forth what is within you,

what you bring forth will save you.

If you do not bring forth what is within you,

what you do not bring forth will destroy you.

—JESUS, THE GOSPEL OF THOMAS

O N A WARM spring day in 1995 the vision came. That day it became clear to Tom Knoblauch and me that, for many reasons, the expressions of love in our world have been shutting down. Perhaps these expressions for some time now have been diminishing, but the broad-sweeping social and environmental effects have recently reached global proportions. From this painful awareness, we discovered deep within ourselves an impulse to assist, with our own abilities and gifts, in opening the doors of love in ourselves and in the world.

We came to the elders in our lives with this vision, hoping that they would help us by offering their wisdom and
deep knowledge of life and love. While we are aware that
the elders in the following dialogues are not fully repre-
sentative of the vast cultural and ethnic diversity of the
general population of American elders, these were our
elders—our friends, colleagues, and mentors. The discussions presented in this book reflect the genuine desire of
all of us to enact love as an offering, to communicate hard-
earned wisdom out of compassion for others, and to
provide a forum for honoring love's role in our lives and
the necessity of continuing to give birth to it in our world.

An elder in our project, Pauline E. Thompson, has suggested that the crucifixion of Christ is symbolic of the
crucifixion of love in the world. This crucifixion represents
our failure to move beyond our own passivity and fear in
order to act on love's behalf, our failure to protect love
from sacrifice in our work settings, our natural environment, our politics, and our intimate relationships. She
contends that our "collective guilt" and depression is that
we continue to remain as spectators while love is crucified
in our daily activities, and that our failure to act is evidence that we have not fully received nor understood
Christ's message of love.

Yet, to act is certainly to move beyond the status quo
and to put oneself "on the line" with regard to the real or
imagined dangers of speaking the truth and engaging
the heart fully in the world. To enact love is no less difficult in this time than it was in Christ's, but it is now,
however, critical to global survival. And we also see that it

is dangerous to our souls not to bring forth and protect that love which is ours to manifest.

With the plethora of psychological and spiritual philosophies available to us, we are often confused about how to position ourselves relative to the worlds of matter and spirit. It is overwhelming, at times, to engage the human experience fully and to imagine that our lives and work might largely be to embody spirit within the world of matter. Love is the essential ingredient that makes it possible for us to remain present and to endure human life's suffering and sober realities. Without love, it is difficult to value our lives; our natural response is detachment from life as a means of coping with its intrinsic physical and emotional pain. If we bring our love forward, after long-standing patterns of safe retreat, we will inevitably upset the comfortable homeostasis of our life situations, and create disturbance and crisis in our usual (and often destructive) ways of adapting to love's absence. Thus, we must be respectful of the potentially overwhelming experience of opening to love's energy when we have sustained unhealthy, yet functional, ways of surviving without it. Our mission, I believe, through the awakening of love, is to discover unique and passionate ways to enter and remain present in the body, in time, in the heart, in creation, and to give birth to our spiritual presence here in the human form.

This project has been an ambitious undertaking. Yet, we feel the extreme importance of bringing forward our intensely felt purpose and responsibility for manifesting love in the world. We also believe that we are unlikely to accomplish this task completely without the involvement, guidance, and blessings of our elders. Therefore, our work is as much an invocation as it is an enactment. We hope that the offerings in this book awaken a deep memory of our origins in love, and that they inspire a re-awakening of the value and importance of Elderhood.

KENNETH R. LAKRITZ

INTRODUCTION

TO BECOME our unique selves rather than second-hand imitations, we need someone standing behind us, saying as it were, "I bless you in the heroic, worthwhile, and difficult task of becoming yourself." Such a person evokes our questing spirit, not by giving answers, but by deepening our ability to question and to search for meaning. As we work through anxiety, doubt, and occasional discouragement in our quest for a genuine life path, our [elder] acts as a midwife, helping us to breathe more easily as we give birth to ourselves in the world.

—ZALMAN SCHACHTER-SHALOMI

THE COURAGE TO ASK THE QUESTION

KENNETH R. LAKRITZ

One day a student came to a rabbi and said,
"In the olden days there were men who saw the
face of God. Why don't they anymore?"
The rabbi replied, "Because nowadays no one is
willing to stoop so low."

— OLD RABBINICAL STORY

ONE OF THOSE self-evident truths is that we live in an ominous time, when our awareness of and ability to express love are critical both to the quality of our lives and to our very survival. I will not recount the difficulties and potential horrors that confront us in our imminent future. Our very predicament soberly confronts us with the challenges of cultivating love in a time of such terrible suffering and pessimism. Andrew Harvey passionately writes:

To birth ourselves into love and let ourselves be birthed by love into itself is why we are here. Our contemporary collective agony is calling us to this great birth on a massive scale. Now more than ever we have to be alive in love . . . to be born into love is the purpose of everything, and embraces all conditions necessary for this splendor, even the most terrible.[1]

Our "collective agony" leads us to look more closely at the crucial issues of our time. It also brings us to ask questions about love that may possibly lead us to appreciate more deeply the awareness and disciplines involved in its expression. While to be born involves a natural gestational process, to be born into a deeper consciousness of love involves humility and a willing and conscious surrender. Our culture thrives on possession and solution, grasping for quick answers and results, and thus we are uncomfortable existing in a state of unknowing, being so accustomed to, and dependent on, gross stimulation and immediate gratification. This is not only a reflection of addiction; it has, culturally, evolved into a position within the person which makes a nonjudgmental and forgiving presence extremely difficult. We must ask ourselves, How can love enter, how can love be born in an environment such as this?

Our predicament also embodies a confrontation with our past and an initiation into a vastly different future. We are awakening to the fact that how we are living, and how we are behaving toward one another, is not working.

As I write, I am aware of my tendency to speak in a philosophical way about the issues facing our world community regarding survival in the twenty-first century. However, today our concerns are highly personal and demand much more from us than abstract philosophical inquiry. I struggle to remain awake to these concerns as they impact me personally. Like many others, I experience a growing appreciation of the mindfulness and disciplines that are involved in living, in practicing a truly loving relationship to life. Increasing awareness of my collusion with a way of life conflicts deeply with my own emerging value of much greater simplicity. Many of us are realizing that we spend much time in vocations without passion and meaning, engaging work predominantly as a means for supporting our expensive lifestyles. We find that we have less and less time to spend with our families, and also less and less time for ourselves. Too often we become so depleted that we are not emotionally available to those we love. Like most of us who share in the increasing complexities and stresses of modern life, I find myself in a way of life with which I know I must cope in order to survive. Yet, I recognize that simply to adapt without questioning or responding conflicts with the deepest core of my heart and feeling of purpose. Once I awaken to my own personal responsibility, I will no longer be able to claim ignorance, and the path ahead will require a deep and refined awareness, a faith, and an irreversible commitment of the heart to fully live-in-life.

I believe that in our American culture we have over-emphasized the intellect, trusting it to guide our whole human conduct. We mistrust and devalue the intuitive wisdom of our hearts. As my heart breaks open to life's painful realities, however, I am learning the importance of surrendering to its deeper mysteries, realizing that I am simply a vessel in which consciousness and love may give birth. The great Sufi master and poet, Rumi, once wrote:

> *A heartbreak shakes the yellow leaves from*
> *the branch of the heart*
> *so fresh leaves can go on growing . . .*
> *Heartbreak pulls up the roots of old happiness*
> *so a new ecstasy can stroll in from beyond.*
> *Heartbreak pulls up all withered, crooked roots*
> *so no root can stay hidden.*
> *Heartbreak may pull many things from the heart*
> *but in return it will lavish kingdoms.*[2]

A good friend once told me a story from his childhood in the interior of Brazil. As a young boy, he was asked by his grandmother to dig for fresh water within an old well where the water had grown dark and stagnant. He recalls digging and digging through the muddy water until he found himself at what appeared to be the bottom of the well. He returned to his grandmother lamenting that he was unable to uncover fresh water within the old stagnant well. She suggested that he continue to dig, although it appeared to him that he would find nothing more than dark mud. So, on her suggestion, he kept on digging. After many hours and days, he lost hope of the possibility of uncovering fresh water and surrendered with a deep feeling of frustration and failure. That night while he lay sleeping, unbeknownst to him, fresh, pure water began to trickle through the mud and to fill the well where the stagnant water once had stood. In the morning when he returned to the well, he was astonished that, at his deepest moment of despair and surrender, the muddy earth gave way and the well was purified and reinvigorated with fresh drinking water.[3]

I believe that this story offers a useful guiding image. Ancient wisdom informs us that through the breaking heart it becomes possible for us to enter into a state of acceptance of not knowing, what the Buddhists have referred to as "beginner's mind." From this humble position we may begin to ask questions, as we ourselves, so to speak, dig in the stagnant well, questions which will reinvigorate our awareness and bring forth a new and fresh understanding.

We cannot will, nor can we dictate, that we become loving individuals. In the evolution of all relationship, love requires our unconscious permission, as well as our conscious willingness, to open our hearts. When we open our hearts, we surrender to an energy and a reality beyond the ego or self. In our surrendering, we open ourselves to possibilities that would otherwise not manifest if we had believed that nothing exists beyond that which can be grasped by the intellect. We can neither birth nor initiate ourselves, and, as Andrew Harvey writes, we must "Let ourselves be birthed by love into itself." From the feminine we must learn about gestation, about holding and growing new life within our hearts, our minds, and our bodies.

For without this deep feminine wisdom, we are vulnerable to abort or miscarry this most precious child who seeks to be born within us.

From this fertile position, in our deeper inquiry into love, we will set aside our preconceived, overworked, uninspired notions about love, and we will begin to ask questions as to its very nature:

- What is love, and what is required of us to cultivate it in our lives?
- What are the barriers that interfere with the awareness and expression of love?
- Where is our confusion and how do we discern between what is and isn't a reflection of love?
- How do we maintain an open, loving heart in the presence of evil, suffering, violence, and hatred?
- Can love be taught and, if so, how?
- What specific disciplines might assist us in manifesting more love in the world?
- Why is our awareness of love so critical at this time?
- What does it mean to put love into action?
- How is love manifested in action and how is this achieved in practical terms?
- What will we need to understand to begin manifesting more love in our lives?

In earlier times, societies valued bringing their concerns and questions to the community of tribal elders.

But today, a breakdown in dialogue between the generations has occurred. While it is unfair to project onto the
elders idealized images—which are confining and actually
inhibit honest and open dialogue—honoring and admiration are very important in cultivating this connection. As
Robert Bly has well articulated, and I also believe, there exists now a wound between elder and youth. Many elders
hold within their hearts a potent and subtle guiding influence as well as a wisdom deepened from life experience.
This wisdom, not born of the intellect, provides a continuity of wisdom from generation to generation. The loss
of dialogue regarding issues such as love is a symptom of
fragmentation. The younger generations bear the responsibility of laboring physically, emotionally, and spiritually
to cultivate a new world, and they are crucially in need
of mature guidance to initiate them into deeper awareness
in the midst of the confusion in their lives. However,
we adults have failed to lead, support, protect, and nurture our young. We expect that they somehow, without
guidance, become more mature than we ourselves are.
Understandably, the resulting lack of trust and contact between generations has created an environment where the
youth are required to initiate themselves.

Members of the younger generations often appear un-
interested in asking questions of the elders, or simply may
not know how to approach them. Perhaps elders no longer
view themselves as integral to the continuity and evolution of the community. One elder who participated in
this discussion exclaimed, "Don't expect much help from
us elders. Most of us have been relegated to retirement

enclosures, golf, bingo, tourism, and uncreative play—
separating ourselves from the problems of the homeless,
the untaught, the unfed." Our elders often exist isolated
in their pain and grief about the ominous future they see
facing themselves and a far more grievous future facing
their children and grandchildren. Feeling unrecognized
for their care and insight, many elders nonetheless would
welcome the opportunity to provide us with very needed
guidance. Much difficulty in transmitting wisdom, however, often results from a tendency to become overly
entangled with the ego or intellect, and, lamentably, some
elders today do not have the kind of wisdom and guidance
we are attempting to evoke. An elder in her nineties,
Pauline Thompson, raised the question: "How can we
honor our parents lovingly or even wisely if they themselves are misunderstood and unloved?"

During the course of our discussions, it became evident
to us that some aspects of the "wisdom of the heart" are
only achieved through time, experience, and discipline.
Rumi once wrote: "Until you have kept your eyes and your
wanting still for fifty years, you don't begin to cross over
from confusion."[4] In today's world, there is certainly
much confusion to overcome, and we require courage and
perspective to remain open-hearted. I was struck by the
consistently held view of the elders in our project that
we teach love by our example and ability to embody and
express love. Those who, through years of struggle and
with a hard-won perspective and peace, have found, as
Joseph Campbell says, "joy among the sorrows of life," are

a precious resource in our world. We often learn that it is truly possible to love life from those who learned to love and embrace all that is involved in living.

Our intent has been to light a flame, to initiate a much-needed dialogue between the generations on a matter so important and central to our existence. We have discovered that there exists in this relationship with elders an energy beyond the context of their words. It is incumbent upon elders to acknowledge the value and power of their blessings, to take seriously the needs of the community for their involvement, and to appreciate the challenges and responsibilities confronting younger generations. Our youth, no doubt, face an increasingly complicated world struggling and suffering through a massive and violent transformation. But the younger generations also have an energy and perspective that is refreshing, hopeful, and alive. This vitality and drive will change the world.

The birth of love is the passageway through to the other side of this transformation. This will not occur by itself and will require our best and wisest midwives, those in whom love has already given birth. We must also recognize that wisdom may come from all stations and ages of life, and not assume that any one person, or persons, has the corner on love or enlightenment. We must remember that each of us are midwives to ourselves and to one another as well. Our future requires that we recognize the beauty of bringing together our differences of age, gender, culture, and wisdom.

T. S. Eliot wrote:

> *We shall not cease from exploration*
> *And the end of all our exploring*
> *Will be to arrive where we started*
> *And know the place for the first time.*[5]

Therefore let us begin by giving love permission to enter, by calling out to love to fill our hearts in response, by giving passionately of ourselves in service, and by continuing to ask questions, so that love may give birth in a world so much in need of its grace.

RE-AWAKENING ELDERHOOD

THOMAS M. KNOBLAUCH

The breeze at dawn has secrets to tell you.
Don't go back to sleep.
You must ask for what you really want.
Don't go back to sleep.
People are going back and forth across the doorsill
where the two worlds touch.
The door is round and open.
Don't go back to sleep.   —RUMI

WITH MANY creative undertakings, one engages the imagination about the pathways necessary to travel during the pursuit of a particular goal. Ken Lakritz and I, psychologists and co-designers of this project, wanted to explore the logic behind seeking out those individuals who are older, who have considerably more life experience than we. We also wanted their help in our search for answers to difficult questions. We agreed to conduct a series of videotaped interviews with a small group of remarkable elders. Our shared initial vision was that these elders would pursue the topics of love, from both religious and secular viewpoints, vigorously and joyfully. Our intention was to conduct a project awakening or re-awakening the understanding of love in the minds and hearts of those who chose to travel this path with us. We saw the potential that interviews such as these have for constituting a method for re-awakening other elders as to their vital importance in an increasingly complex world. We also felt the need to re-examine the elder's traditional role in initiating the young to full adulthood, because of our concerns about the decline of this role.

As this project developed, we were able to appreciate how it became a social experiment for us all, an open invitation for these elders to engage in a dialogue in which might be shared deep recollections of the passage of the human spirit throughout life. For this project, we were fortunate to recruit seven elders whom we had the good fortune to know personally or meet by way of recommendations from friends. To gather such a diverse group and to witness these elders' participation in it turned out to be a unique experience for us all.

Our invitation to these elders is similar to the one given by Robert Lawlor to his readers in *Voices of the First Day* where he offers the encouragement "to enter, as in a dream, a lost memory of our race as well as a fresh imagining of the earth's cycles of death and rebirth." Lawlor's plea is not for the return to an aboriginal hunter-gatherer way of life, but rather for participation in activities of re-visioning the possibilities for renewing the dignity and mystery of human life.

> Dreams, deep collective memories, and imaginings are more potent than religious faith or scientific theories in lifting us above the otherwise catastrophic ending that confronts us all. A recollection of our origins—a remembrance of a sense of reality in its pure and primary form—is essential if we are to understand our present circumstance and imagine the possibilities of our collective destiny.[1]

Several years ago I read an article in a small town newspaper about elementary school curricula and the types of books for various grade levels. A fifth-grade reader entitled *Knock at the Door* was highly recommended for a story entitled "Words from a Grandfather," about the Native American Indian Chief Dan George. As an elder, he spoke to the younger members of his tribe: "Perhaps there will be a day you will want to sit by my side asking my counsel. I hope I will be there, but you see I am growing old. There is no promise that life will live up to our hopes, especially to the hopes of the aged. So I write what I know and some day our hearts will meet in these words—if you let it happen." The phrase "if you let it happen" is repeated throughout his entreaty to the younger generation. At the end of Chief Dan George's speech to his people, the school reader outlines questions for the students on the topic of elders, such as, "Why are elders important to us?" and "Who are some elders in your world?"[2]

Many of us were taught to "respect our elders" yet we lacked a deeper understanding of exactly why we should do so. We did not receive specific instruction about the skills, knowledge, or heritage our elders could give us. And, regrettably, many of us were unable to identify our elders, especially those beyond the boundaries of our immediate families.

We recognized the fact that we are two psychologists in mid-life who are seeking to move beyond our day-to-day work as therapists and consultants. Feeling the need for a transition to a new level of providing service in our own lives, we wanted to move beyond the old methods of problem-solving in order to broaden our understanding of human consciousness. We were discovering in our daily work with patients and fellow mental health workers that the element of love was missing. Yes, there were loving, caring persons around us, but there was a noticeable absence of a general loving atmosphere in which to assist people with conflicts and suffering. It was as if the dimensions of the heart, of the human spirit, were not brought into awareness as a means of helping people.

Working in a healthcare delivery-system with its inherent complexities and inevitabilities takes a toll on its providers. Such a system serves as a breeding ground for stress disorders, substance-abuse problems, and depression. We faced the painful realization that we, too, were potential victims of powerful institutional demands, and that, for the sake of our own well-being, we needed to strive toward a new model of engaging others in our work as clinicians. We, too, were sometimes subject to the phenomenon of "learned helplessness"—losing the manifestation of our full potential because of organizational pressures and limitations. Under such stress-filled conditions, one can easily "fall asleep" or surrender to a type of personal amnesia regarding earlier dreams and passions.

We were faced, moreover, with a sense of isolation. Not many therapists seemed to be moving to a new level of practice in our craft. In the broader culture, we knew that we had mentors—people such as Robert Bly, Ram Dass, Andrew Harvey, Matthew Fox, and James Hillman—who were themselves attempting to develop new ways of understanding issues such as community, spirituality, healing, and love. Within our immediate work environment, however, we could find no true mentors or elders. Consequently, we found ourselves in a predicament: We sought to make a substantial transition in our own lives yet were lacking the necessary guidance to do so. Determined to move into that transition phase, we sought out elders in our midst who might provide a true entry way into our new work.

And as psychologists seeking positive passage through midlife ourselves, and as aspirants in midlife, we sought a foothold in the elders' experience. We were seeking to cross over from one identity rooted in age to another. Murray Stein, in his book *In Midlife,* used the myth of the Greek god Hermes to explain the drama and "crisis of the spirit" which is at the core of midlife transition. The god, whose sense of timing is critical in bringing messages from beyond to those in crisis, travels between the human realm and that of the divine.[3] We need our own Hermes to strengthen the lines of communication between the generations.

In her introduction to *Betwixt and Between,* Louise Carus Mahdi underscores the fact that we are in a period of "initiation hunger" because modern civilization has lost the collective rites of times past.[4] She points to the need for elders "who themselves have been initiated." In addition, she emphasizes the importance of working with others in groups, as well as in one-to-one dialogues, as a means of compensating for what has been lost. She highlights the work of A. Stevens, who comments on the absence of initiation in our culture:

> Society at large has abdicated responsibility for initiating the young. Traditional initiatory procedures have been allowed to atrophy with disuse because our "elders" have lost confidence in the values of which they are the custodians and no longer possess any certain knowledge as to what it might be that they are initiating young people for. Ultimately, it is the fault of neither teacher nor pupil, elder nor novice, but the consequence of a collective crisis of confidence in our culture.[5]

James Hillman, a strong voice for those wishing to "revision" psychology, uses the Jungian concepts of *senex,* the Wise Old Man, and *puer,* the Eternal Youth, to point out the considerable ambivalence of our attempts to deal emotionally with elders. In effect, we fail to integrate the two poles represented by the puer and senex archetypes. We need a harmonious sense of both youth and old age, either from our "internal" psychological standpoint or in an "external" integration of young and old in the culture. In *Puer Papers,* Hillman comments on the widespread divisions between young and old:

> A polar division between senex and puer is all about us, outside in the historical field. We find good example of this in demography, which has reached back to an archaic system: peoples are again divided along lines of age and youth . . . youth forms a social class, self-enclosed and uninitiated by its elders, and thus largely without communication outside of itself.[6]

Hillman emphasizes that we cannot, in fact, have a proper sense of personal or social history without the young and old coming together to share in the telling and recollecting of past events. Youth needs tellers; elders need listeners. Elders may possess wisdom, yet today they are often viewed with suspicion and fear by the young. The act of surrendering oneself to initiation may be a painful "leap of faith" for the young person, and trust is necessary in order to accept the elder's role in the formation of the new identity.

In designing this particular social experiment, we did not consciously say to ourselves, "We need to go to our elders for initiation." The process was more gradual. We knew the majority of the participants in our project and already trusted them as mentors, teachers, and friends. We did not turn to them for personal assistance or for individual instruction on furthering ourselves as therapists; we went to them as members of our entire culture. We voiced, as it were, a call from our collective world, asking, "Help us. How can we share love? How can we make love more influential in our world?"

In our examination of love as a potential healing, transformative force in the culture at large, we approached these mentors accompanied by our own sense of growing personal authority, our own emerging eldership. We did not ask these elders to "fill us up," as if we were empty containers seeking basic instruction; we asked for dialogue.

We selected individuals who themselves had been initiated in a number of different ways throughout their lifetimes. While they agreed to discuss their views about love, they in no way implied that they had definitive answers to either the personal problems or ills of modern society. Instead, they simply agreed to record their experiences.

This project can also be seen as an application of a new model for Elderhood that Zalman Schachter-Shalomi outlines in his book *From Age-ing to Sage-ing®*. He points out that the model of human development based on aging ends in a state of personal decline and intellectual and emotional impoverishment, wherein the individual becomes less engaged with the world toward the end of life. As an alternative to this negative "inevitable senescence," he proposes a model of late-life development called "sage-ing," whereby older people are enabled to become "spiritually radiant, physically vital, and socially respon-sible 'elders of the tribe.'" His new psychology of aging would transform the notion of a downward spiral toward death into an upward "arc of expanded consciousness," which would "crown the elder's life with meaning and purpose." [7]

For Schachter-Shalomi the use of the media can be in-strumental in changing our present "cultural aging script." Television, for example, might be used as a tool for creating programming that show elders as positive role models "engaged in creative activity that benefits so-ciety." He reflects on the possibilities:

> "In the near future, we might tune in on Sunday evening to a program entitled Elder Heroes," says Doug Waldo, who hosted *Seniors Speak Out,* a program for the over-fifty audience that was produced for seven years at KPBS, San Diego's public television station. "The program would feature exemplary elders —the Maggie Kuhns of the world—who are making a difference in people's lives by giving of themselves. Such programs can use mass communications to stim-ulate public dialogue in an attempt to reassimilate the wisdom of elders in society." [8]

While we consider the elders we chose "exemplary," there are elders in the midst of the daily lives of everyone who embody untapped knowledge and wisdom. We must not be drawn away from our immediate community by heralding more visible, more renowned individuals. Robert Fleming discusses the issue of the role of elders in African-American culture:

> We spend our time calculating how we can be smarter, richer, and more successful, while turning away from the gold mine in our midst. We go to therapists, psychics, and hypnotists, instead of picking up the phone to call Aunt Bessie or Uncle Silas. One day we will be asked to pass our wisdom on to those who follow us in the same way that our honored forebears once passed on their values, customs, and time-honored strengths to our generation. We cannot be the broken link in this chain. We must return to that light of wisdom that burns so brightly among us. We must draw on the nourishing warmth of our elders' presence before it is lost to us.[9]

The seven elders were not interviewed as gurus. While we recognize that they may have some spiritual authority, we do not intend to create any aggrandizement of their abilities.

Part of what we all discovered during the course of our discussions is how simple, direct, immediate, and yet powerful are the questions, "How are you doing?" and "How can I be of help to you?" Ram Dass and Paul Gorman devote their entire book *How Can I Help?* to the stories of ordinary people providing selfless service to others. They interviewed a ninety-two-year-old man who rises each morning as an "Honorary Sanitation Commissioner" to alert his neighbors to remove their cars from a city street prior to the arrival of the street sweepers. This man reflects on the service he offers his community:

> What can I tell you? I'm not a saint or a wise man. I'm not the Two-Thousand-Year-Old Man, I'm only the ninety-two-year-old man. Just a senior citizen. But what do I know that everybody else doesn't know? We know. I just go out there in the morning and blow my whistle. That's what I do. Me, I'm having a great time. Wonderful fun. And when people see how much fun I'm having, they have to laugh. What else can they do? Then I hit them with it: "Move your car!" [10]

An important aspect of this ninety-two-year-old's wisdom is his seizing of an opportunity to provide a service to another person, choosing to provide this unsolicited service, offered without obligation.

Initially, we had in mind the development of a video project through which we would provide individual families the opportunity to interview elder family members about their lives, striving to help them bring forward pertinent memories relative to the history of their particular extended family or clan. We thought of titling this endeavor "The Legacy Project." We were intrigued by the idea of a service which could be provided to families in which family members could ask their elders key questions, questions which might assist them in examining and summarizing their lifetimes, and pass on important knowledge and values to their descendants. Being able to answer the question, "Where have we been?" before considering "Where are we going?" is basic to the extension of human existence.

Of these seven elders, we asked a question critical to us: "Can you teach people to be loving?" No consensus was reached, yet there was agreement that there may be ways to develop the capacity to love. Certainly, if we can remember what it feels like to be loving toward another, then we can use that memory. Furthermore, if we can develop some awareness of how our egos get in the way, we can allow the human spirit to fill the heart.

If our elders can teach us something of use to ourselves or humanity, then we need to enter into an ongoing relationship with them. Perhaps projects such as this one represent an example of what might be called "the technology of remembering." We have seen how the simple process of just sitting down to talk with each other can provide an awakening to a way of being that has been forgotten. The use of recall and recollection may also bring ourselves more fully into the present moment. While this is not a new idea, the use of video recorders facilitates recall and provides the means of "playback" for important memories.

Historians inform us that transmission of knowledge throughout the ages occurred primarily as the result of the oral tradition, the handing down of songs and stories from one generation to the next. An entire issue of PARABOLA Magazine was devoted to the importance of keeping the oral tradition alive as a primary method of transmitting subtle layers of meaning. In his essay entitled "The Call to Remember," Arthur Amiotte recalls the Native American elders from his childhood who helped him appreciate the importance of words and "naming things" during the course of an initiatory ritual:

> Ritual on this level serves to focus the minds and memories of the participants upon a specific significant event and its implications for becoming what the culture prescribes as a "good person." The attending actions, songs, and orations, done with feeling and sincerity, make a profound impression on the being of the central person. He in turn is admonished to *remember* the all-important condition for retention of *Lakol Wicoha* (the Lakota traditions), and incorporation of his own life story into that of his people, their history and ideals.[11]

While we began by asking our participants to bring forth personal recollections, some of us ended with the sense that we were working together toward the realization of a much deeper memory or possibly serving as a conduit for a much deeper species-wide remembrance. Yet the end result of our discussions was also to leave us with a greater sense of what our task as human beings is—the dissemination of hope and understanding.

In its way, deeper memory is a personal "covenant," a

sense of bringing forth commitment, or accessing personal law. Love can be seen as one's covenant, as the ultimate covenant that we can have in this life: to love ourselves, our parents, our families, our friends, our neighbors, and God (in whatever form that idea takes).

Throughout our conversations, we all agreed that the absence of love can have devastating consequences. We even agreed that there is tremendous power in showing people the smallest amount of attention, and understood how people can lose their way in a life where they do not receive the proper acknowledgment of personal worth. Providing others simple gestures of encouragement cannot be taken for granted. In her book, *Tales of the Elders,* Carol Ann Bates presents the stories of men and women who came to America as immigrants. One elder recalls the importance of blessing in his father's life:

> My father often spoke of the importance of honesty and maintaining a good name. His guiding principles for the family were obedience, loyalty, love, respect, and honorable actions at all times. I recall one lesson he taught me about respect. When entering the home, we children were expected to greet our father and all other elders with the saying *Vossia mi benedica,* "Give me your blessing." But after a few years in America I began to think that this was old-fashioned, and one day I refused to say it. My father ordered me out of the house and told me to come back only when I was prepared to enter like a Christian. I waited outside, somewhat rebellious. I tried to enter again without

saying those words and was sent out again. Finally, after freezing on the back porch for a while, I entered and dutifully said, "Vossia mi benedica." My father responded, *"Dio ti benedice,"* "God will bless you." [12]

In the past, the way of things was absolute acceptance and surrender to the authority of elders. Now, we are living in a time when the notion of adhering to custom or (as some would say) surrendering to another seems abhorrent, when there is freedom to question authority, when no young person accepts carte blanche the wisdom of his or her seniors. But many young people do not have the means or the mature ability to evaluate whether or not a particular piece of advice will be good for them. Perhaps we need to understand that the issue isn't so much one of mindless obedience to authority, but rather seeing the power behind attending to others as a means of securing aid in transition to effective old age.

In *The Sibling Society,* Robert Bly looks at our society's widespread self-absorption and lack of spiritual direction. He speculates that we have become people who have refused to grow up and who are neglecting the important duty of preparing the next generation to take its inevitable place in the world. In addition, he believes that the media have colluded in failing to provide young people with proper elder role models who can help them with the task of coming to age. In an interview with Richard Simon, he reflects on what he believes has happened to our culture:

The point . . . is to make people feel how shipwrecked

our society is, so that they would start thinking of things themselves. But I think we have to recover something I call vertical attention, which is not the same thing as hierarchy. Since the 1960s, we've been busy destroying authority, thinking that will make us more free. But what we've done is to flatten things. We've done away with the old awe and respect for the nonhuman world, the seven heavens above us and the demons below us. It's one thing to do away with the old power hierarchies that oppressed people, but we've also done away with the longing for the divine. That longing for the divine led Bach, led Mirabai, led Emerson to amazing places. We've replaced that longing for spiritual transcendence with our awe of the computer . . .

So what we look for is the food that can feed our longing. We could say that vertical longing is one of the few weapons we have to use against the constant greed of the body, wanting to eat more, possess more.[13]

Robert Bly also accuses many elders themselves of not growing up, of wanting to retire and settle into their own brand of self-indulgent entitlement without accountability. The message he and others give is that we need to continue growing up, even in old age. We need to press our lasting abilities into service, to put love into action. To accomplish this, we must learn how to recognize the special gifts or potential of each person and to assist each other in finding our own useful roles in life.

We must actively create intergenerational dialogues if we are to move harmoniously into our collective destiny as a human race. The coming generations need to learn the intricacies of heart-mind-body-spirit integration as they have been experienced by people who have already lived into the last phase of their lives. What our elders can offer us today is remembered experience in our joint struggle with these mysteries.

For us, these explorations have been fruitful. The simple joy and stimulating pleasure of our brief time together are gifts we now invite others to share.

ELDERS ON LOVE

When love beckons you follow him,
Though his ways are hard and steep.
And when his wings enfold you yield to him,
Though the sword hidden among his pinions
may wound you.
And when he speaks to you believe in him,
Though his voice may shatter your dreams
as the north wind lays waste the garden.
For even as love crowns you so shall it crucify you.
Even as he is for your growth so is he for your pruning.
Even as he ascends to your height and
caresses your tenderest branches that quiver in the sun,
so shall he descend to your roots and shake them
in their clinging to the earth.
Like sheaves of corn he gathers you unto himself.
He threshes you to make you naked.
He sifts you to free you from your husks.
He grinds you to whiteness.
He kneads you until you are pliant;
And then he assigns you to his sacred fire,
that you may become sacred bread for God's sacred feast.

—KAHLIL GIBRAN

TIMOTHY CROCKER

The freedom that is our nature is our ability to
love something, someone besides ourselves, and
for the sake, not of ourselves, but of the one we
love. . . . This power to love another for his
own sake is one of the things that makes us like
God, because this power is the one thing in us
that is free from all determination. It is a power
which transcends and escapes the inevitability of
self-love.

—THOMAS MERTON

To love is to be in communion with the other
and to discover—in that other—
the spark of God.

—PAULO COELHO

TIMOTHY CROCKER

WAS BORN in 1920 in Barranquilla, Columbia, where my parents were missionaries of the Presbyterian Church. When Dad came down with tropical infections our missionary life ended, and we returned to my grandparents' home in Minnesota and then moved to California for his convalescence. He committed suicide at age sixty when I was twenty-seven years old.

During my youth in San Diego, California, we started an Oxford Movement group with our school friends and neighbors. Later this became significant to me because during that same period Bill Wilson, co-founder of A.A., began his sobriety in Oxford Movement gatherings in New York.

I entered medical school at the University of California, San Francisco (UCSF) in 1941. I graduated in 1944 as a member of the Medical Student Honor Society and was awarded the Gold Headed Cane of the UCSF School of Medicine. (Each year I meet with The Gold Headed Cane Society to honor candidates for the year's "caning.") My residencies at UCSF were in pathology and internal medicine. Afterwards, as a captain in the U.S. Army Medical Corps I did virus research at Walter Reed Army Medical Center. Then, after two years of research and medical residency training at Yale University Medical School, I was appointed a Markle Foundation Medical

Scholar at UCSF as Assistant Professor of Medicine in 1950 at age thirty. With an added appointment to the Cancer Research Institute my work turned to the biology of intracellular infections and then to the effects of carcinogens in polluted air and cigarette smoke. After I was awarded a Guggenheim Foundation Fellowship, I spent a sabbatical year at Cambridge, England. I returned to UCSF, and then moved in 1971 to be Professor and Chairman of the Department of Community and Environmental Medicine at the University of California, Irvine, College of Medicine. After 1990 I worked at Napa State Hospital as a physician and surgeon with qualifications as an epidemiologist in Occupational Medicine and Public Health.

During my residency at UCSF I married Miriam Dyer-Benet, then a student nurse. Our children are Edith, Stephen, Thomas, and Cedric. Miriam and I became estranged and we divorced in 1961. After ten years of single life, I married Kathleen Conrey in 1971. She urged me to stop drinking and she joined me in attending A.A. as of March 15, 1972, which was my first "sobriety date." We had seven sober years before we separated in 1979. I married Beryl, a psychiatric social worker, in 1989 and then moved to Napa.

And now after my second retirement, I feel ready to enjoy full time the life of traveling, reading, recovery, and family activities.

TOM: I'd like to welcome you to our series "Elders On Love." Dr. Crocker, you've been so gracious to join us. Today I'd like to talk about love, about its meaning in your life, about teaching love, and about bringing it into a broader context of spirituality and community.

TIM: Tom, I'm grateful to be here. This topic, as you describe it, has caused me a fair amount of breast-beating and interior examination, because of its scope and profundity. Love is probably a subject that is most critical to our survival, certainly to my survival, personally. I am honored to be invited to do this, but I'm burdened.

TOM: What is it that was burdensome for you when you were thinking about this topic?

TIM: Well, for one thing, the sense of love's being a very profound topic. I probably have never fully experienced it in my own life, and, to the extent that I have, that I might not be able to articulate it has left me feeling a little dumb in the face of a topic of such scope. At the same time, I felt that it was my obligation to be as clear and concise as possible in my description of love and its influence in my life, in the belief that it would do someone some good. And then I suddenly came to realize that this sense of tremendous responsibility and obligation was just one more ego trip, which may be the reason why love is hard to live, because it interferes with its expressions.

TOM: What you're saying is that if we approach this topic from the perspective of ego, then we haven't furthered our understanding of love. Do you think that's a fair statement?

TIM: Certainly—if we think that love and ego are

connected. There is a certain self-love that is within the practice of egoism, but it's only in overcoming and transcending that self-love that love becomes a phenomenon of my life that isn't just egocentric. I think we begin as infants with a sense of self-love in which the only object in our awareness is ourselves and our needs. That's an appropriate survival experience for the infant until the time it comes to realize its dependence upon the mother, to know there is a kind of wonder in the availability of the mother, and to begin to love the mother. But the infant's loving is almost an extension of its own self-love; it feels itself requiring the mother and, because of its own self-interest, it may find itself loving this source. We all have had a very real experience of attachment. There's a difference between love and attachment, for instance. In some ways, I haven't really come to know that difference. And there is a very profound connection between love and attachment because, in many cases, our attachment is a situation in which we believe there should be love—for example, for our parents. Such attachment is not something I can escape, but it is not necessarily a love bond. It's something more of an obligation, an obligatory bond. Self-love is an important idea for us to consider, but as a means to know that it is not the love that I seek or that we all ultimately find in the love of others.

TOM: How did you become aware of this distinction between love and attachment?

TIM: The issue of attachment, especially of infants and children towards their parents, is an unavoidable process that must always happen and does happen. The caregiver is a very vital influence in the life of the child. So the loss of attachment, and the fear of the loss of attachment, are some of the most critical fears that we have as children. Often that loss of attachment or the experience of a loss of attachment creates a bitter and cynical response in the child as the feeling of having been betrayed or deserted. As a result, hate may develop instead of love. The outcome may indeed be the bitter child who no longer loves the parent and is living in a life of betrayal, a very uncomfortable place in which to be. So while attachment and love may not be the same, the withdrawal of the bond that nurtures attachment may lead to hate. Now hate is not the opposite of love. I think indifference is the opposite of love. Hate still represents a terribly powerful bond, a love bond that's unkind, that's being picked up from the dark side. So attachment has to do with survival and the need for connection, and is simply a part of our childhood experience, and somehow it relates to love but it is not love.

TOM: There are a number of issues that you're bringing up here. I'd like to start with this notion of love and attachment. Do you think that people in their relationships try to get back to some feeling of love that they had in childhood?

TIM: I have a kind of longing for connection that I regard as precious, immensely valuable, and which almost always involves a figure that is either a woman or someone like a father figure or a saintly figure, someone who personifies the things that I value highly and, therefore, there is a quality of a search. I don't think that I knew earlier I had this sense of search. I now look back upon the longing in my youth as a longing that could not be fulfilled or expressed only in sex. It was a highly idealized kind of longing. It often led to moments of tremendous joy and inward feelings of reward when an experience of some kind of warm, powerful leadership came from another person and directed itself upon me.

As I look back, I remember having this wonderful feeling of a bond between myself and either a person or the group that I was part of. This kind of peak experience usually came in a context that was semi-religious and, as I look back on it, I found that that quality of joy and exaltation that I had at that time was essentially what I was looking for. It could be called love. I not only felt connected to the situation or person but honored to be in that connection.

TOM: You talked initially about how one can interfere with the expression of love. What do you see as the possible barriers to love, in society and in individual people, that prevent us from being in a true place of love and loving?

TIM: I don't know if I can speak for mankind. I can only speak for myself. I know that the barriers for me are self-absorption, a kind of egocentricity, a care for only my concerns, a feeling of indifference to the experiences of others. For me, to have the feeling or experience of love is to be in the presence of others in the way that allows me to experience my concerns for how they are. It's very important to me in my marriage, for example, to be able to hear and understand, without trying to fix things that come up between us. The very practice of doing things for the home is a joy. Another person or other people must be there for me to live with love, because love is not something that I particularly experience by myself. The barrier is, therefore, an unwillingness to be present among others in a way that gives me a chance to hear, understand, empathize, and find compassion with what is happening in their lives.

TOM: Is there a way that we can teach others how to shift from a place of being self-centered to being more loving?

TIM: The only way that I have seen that happening is when someone reaches a point of desperation, despair, an internal pit, a point at which there is apparently no way up except by some power other than themselves. At that point, the power of the care of others can bring them from that pit into a sense of hope. I don't know if anyone ever says to oneself, "I'm going to get up this morning and I'm going to go and be loving." Instead it's "I'm going to get up this morning, I'm despairing, and I'm going to have to do something about this." Then, one finds a way to do something by taking this despair to others. Letting others in a group share their former despair and their subsequent relief from it gives that person a sense of hope. That hope is realized not entirely from the group itself, but from the discovery by the person of a higher power within. There is where the basis and experience of love, it seems to me, must come from. I don't know whether there is a doctrine of love that's acceptable at all. I think love is something that I have to experience, and I may not bring myself to experience it unless it's the only way out of desperation.

TOM: What makes waking up and saying, "I'm going to be a loving person today," difficult?

TIM: The reason is because love is unselfish, love is patient, love is accepting, love is without expectations. Why would anybody want to become all these things because of some brief whim, thinking that this state of love would be a nice place in which to be? I somehow feel that we acquire love only when it's the only way out of the place where we have been, a place which is somehow no longer tenable. We may need to be somewhere else. I think we may not even know that. I think that falling in love is very often a feeling of one's own incompleteness and the need for someone else to fill one. In the case of love between a man and woman, love may be a very beautiful description of that feeling of incompleteness and the need to be fulfilled. But I have the feeling that love is a more general love for others rather than sexual attraction, and is the love that we will find in brotherhood, sisterhood, fellowship, and shared support of one another. That love which can transform the way that I behave in my overall living, and not just the way I behave towards a woman, is the love that I believe will be the solution to the world's ills, which are based largely on self-centered motives of greed, power, and desire for control and mastery of others.

TOM: I wonder if you could comment on how we haven't, as a society, managed to appreciate or share that value of transformative love.

TIM: I am saddened to realize that one of the places where that experience happens to many men is in the army. The quality of brotherhood does occur there, because the whole body of men is brought together to confront an enemy who brings a mortal hazard. When they are in that condition, a fellowship and brotherhood do emerge. I have often wondered whether man's attraction to war is partly the consequence of the bond that occurs among men when they are in the face of an enemy. Very often in war we find that the whole country experiences a change of mood, a general increase in sympathy, generosity, open-heartedness. During the Second World War, I remember there was a great deal more of a community spirit of shared experience, common concern for the welfare of us all. This was not a moment of widespread love, necessarily, but it was a time of the kind of behavior among people that I think love might very well bring. It's unfortunate that it seems to happen in the face of a common enemy.

TOM: It seems, though, that we have common enemies now. It might be war against poverty or hunger, or for environmental issues. But you don't see these issues bringing us together in the way that you've just described.

TIM: Yes, unfortunately, I think it may be because we all have our different enemies. In this case, we do not all agree that poverty is our enemy, or, for that matter, immensely powerful international corporations or the media. Each of us has his or her own enemy. Those who encounter a common enemy form groups. There are groups that are concerned for the Napa River or for the homeless or the poor. There are, of course, the political groups in which there is presumably some devotion to a political platform, which is supposed to benefit one or another view of life. Wherever groups form, there may be brotherhood and the evolution of some of the manifestations of love. But we don't all share the same enemy, except in war. In this case, the war must be generally approved of, because the Vietnam War, for example, did not have this effect upon us as a people. It created dissension among us Americans as to the validity and appropriateness of the conflict, whereas there was not such unrest over our participation in the Second World War. So war, as such, doesn't necessarily create the experience of fellowship.

The element of love is a sort of byproduct of our joining together to do anything, but it most often happens that we join together to oppose something we find inappropriate. The loyalty and personal devotion that people have given to political parties, for example, where they think they are sharing a common objective, is immense. So they may be experiencing love or are simply experiencing brotherhood in a common cause. But I believe they are coming as close to the experience of love as they may ever be. Therefore, I don't think that when I rise in the morning and say, "I will now be loving," it will work for me. But if I rise in the morning and say, "I will now join my buddies in the course of opposing those forces that we are totally against," I may rise from my bed with great anger at our common enemy, without knowing that I've got a sort of loving attachment to my brothers.

TOM: I think it might be difficult for someone else to perceive love in that intention, given what you're saying.

TIM: It might, it might indeed. Although it comes to the giving of life as a part of loyalty to the group. People in such groups do give their lives for the group. Thus, the old postulate, that greater love hath no man than to give his life for another, is something that group members do experience.

TOM: We're trying with this series to ask the elder generation to speak directly to the younger generations about love. We want to offer you the opportunity to speak about what you see as some key issues about love or values that you feel are important.

TIM: I'm aware that almost nothing older people say reaches younger people, nor would it have reached me when I was young. Anything other than describing my own experience would be hollow, because I don't have a message other than the story of my own experience. If I tried to give a message that came out of principle or ideals, it would have the same non-effect on the young as it had on me when older people told me what their ideals were. If, on the other hand, I see someone who, as an older person, attracts me and elicits my respect and ultimately my love, I may find that I model myself after someone who is older. I did this as a young person because of the qualities that person displayed, not because of the things that person said. For example, I had a fabulous love for Franklin D. Roosevelt who was a strong, witty, humorous, assertive leader. I originally had a background of tremendous opposition to him because my family was absolutely incensed about his becoming president. But I found him gracious and powerful, influencing the life of the country for the better, and I found that I loved him. If I were to have found myself pursuing a course of life that was loving, it was because I said, "Yes, I agree with this older person and what he's bringing us to." Thus, the elder can be a source of influence on the younger.

TOM: Let's take FDR as an example. What do you think he represented to you?

TIM: He represented a commitment to alleviate the problems of many people in the desperate situation of the Depression, with their loss of dignity that came with the loss of work. He gave people work. He gave people meaningful work, in many cases, because he gave them work that they would have sought. He set up organizations that would provide work at all levels, from the level of the advanced artist to the level of a young person who could do no more than shovel. But he gave work to people that gave them a sense of participating or contributing to life, and in many cases such work was done in organizations or groups. The CCC, Civilian Conservation Corps, for example, had many of the same internal benefits as the Army does. The Army membership is full of conflict, of course, and there are disputes and there are grumblings in any army. But the Conservation Corps created a place in which young people worked together and could do things that they knew how to do, or, happy to learn, they could be easily taught. Roosevelt was, therefore, a creator of dignity, of opportunity, of hope. These are qualities, I think, of love. When we can give people the experiences of these qualities, that's a loving act.

TOM: Do you see any of our leaders today embodying some of these same qualities?

TIM: The first that comes to mind is the Dalai Lama. His whole following, especially his Tibetan Buddhist family, is under immense pressure from outside, from the Chinese. Yet he radiates love, hope, and does not even express antipathy or anger toward the Chinese government. He simply expresses hope that they may be allowed to see differently. If anyone were expressing love in a most unusual place to be loving, in the presence of this kind of fragmentation and pressure from outside, in spite of what I could only call miserable repression, the Dalai Lama is the one man I can imagine who can maintain a pure face of love.

TOM: How do you imagine that he does that? What do you think goes into the making of someone like that? What kind of discipline is entailed or required to hold that posture?

TIM: I can't speak for him, but I do know that he follows a practice of daily meditation. Very often the meditation is to permit himself to be free of all thoughts, not only angry thoughts, but all thoughts. He also practices a meditation in which he experiences or voices within himself compassion towards all persons, not only as friends, not only as subjects, not only as adherents, but toward his enemies as well. He undertakes that practice every day, and he even leads others in that practice. The practice of such emptiness, such removal from the pressures of all things, is in effect to accept all things, and love does that. Love accepts all things. It is a life of acceptance, but also, as in the case of the Dalai Lama, a life of personal expression and giving of hope and dignity to others. He accepts all things including his own faults, our faults, the faults of the Chinese or others. Then, on top of that, he teaches us how we may reach that position ourselves and experience hope. I have the feeling that he is perhaps the most active living example of a life of loving.

TOM: Would you recommend that we might teach more compassion, or encourage more meditation as a society, or is that too simplistic?

TIM: I can only speak again from an experience. I was traveling in Thailand, which is a country that values Buddhism very highly; there is a very widespread support of the Buddhist priesthood and of Buddhist institutions. But I don't know how many of the people of the country themselves practice meditation. Very often in such a society those who do practice it, do so for us all. Therefore, we honor the practice through them and support them, even to the point, as in Thailand, of filling their begging bowls when they go forth at mid-day to have them filled. Our respect for that practice may be expressed only in our giving to it, not in our doing it ourselves.

TOM: That's very interesting. It almost sounds like a portion of society is let off the hook because people know that they have an institution of meditators or compassionate people who are doing the work.

TIM: You wonder if that may not be so. Many have

been impressed with the friendliness, the general hospitality of everyone in Thailand's culture as though something in the culture is an expression of the modesty, dignity, and generosity of the priesthood. It's as though the priests were there to do what we all admire and wish to do, and as though this were somehow a culture-wide attitude and outlook. Many have also spoken, for example, of the generosity and hospitality of the common people of Tibet who are not monks or nuns, who receive strangers and give help, and who have an open, generous, friendly, happy attitude. There is a quality of internal goodness among the people who are part of a culture in which the meditation and the practice of an outlook of compassion and peace is highly regarded.

TOM: How about political leaders in our society? Is there anyone you can think of that embodies these qualities you're talking about?

TIM: I think the most outstanding of our current leaders is Jimmy Carter. Here's a man at an older stage of life who expresses constructive, compassionate, outward thoughtfulness and mindfulness of the needs of mankind, the oppressed, and of people in conflict. I regard him with general and genuine veneration. I think of him as a splendid example in our current culture and time. He influences me by what he does, not by what he says. I don't find that any doctrine will reach me, but example will.

TOM: So it's action?

TIM: It's action. I'm grateful that the media are giving him what visibility they do, though I think they give a limited visibility to his actions. I think the media give limited opportunity to see what good has been done in Haiti and how both Clinton and Carter have contributed to the present state of some quiet in that country.

TOM: How about the role of the media in terms of teaching about love?

TIM: I wouldn't change the media. I expect the media are responding to what they believe is wanted by the people. So when the media report on crime, violence, disaster, they are somehow reflecting the interest of us all in this, but I find myself feeling that there is a good deal of good news that goes on that we are not recognizing. I think even when the good news is victory in the Olympics, we take that victory as sort of an ego gratification rather than the joy over the quality of competition and the high athleticism of participants. The media might very well tell more about what's good in Haiti than they have. There are many opportunities for the media to describe events that are, I would say, loving events. There's one television program called "911" which depicts rescue efforts by firemen, emergency medical technicians, and ordinary citizens who participate in the saving of a life or limb of someone in disaster or danger. These stories conclude with the gathering together of the saved and the savers who find themselves bonded in a very friendly, loving way. That program describes an outright gift of energy, effort, and goodwill to rescue someone in difficulty and the experience afterwards of a carrying forward of the brotherhood of that experience. The rescuers are wholehearted, and the reception at the end of the event seems wholehearted and generous.

TOM: I think the selflessness that's involved in these rescue efforts is admirable.

TIM: It's an example that is to the media's credit. Someone finds this to be good material for programming in television, and I believe it is. One area where Americans do, indeed, give love in a public way, is in emergencies. We're very good at rescues, but we aren't good at indefinite continuation of helping those who need help on a long-term basis. We're ready for war; we're ready for fire; we're ready for disaster; and we've got wonderful equipment and well-trained people to respond to these crises.

TOM: What you're saying is true. The day-to-day work of being in relationships at work, at home, and in the family, with their subtle challenges, is very different from the demands these disasters and tragedies might involve.

TIM: I think many fellowships have grown out of a rescue function, which has brought people back from the brink of despair and disaster to a state of hope. But the people who are in such fellowships continue to meet even long after they are rescued and to practice a kind of giving and acts of love which influence and are part of the way they live now, not just the way they got over their serious difficulty. In these fellowships may be people who had their recovery, their beginnings, years before, but who still participate in the rescue of others who come in need. They maintain a fellowship of gratitude for their recovery and of gratitude for their continuing lifestyle, and a rein-forcement of that lifestyle which does permit relationships to be regarded as dear obligations.

TOM: What you're describing is an atmosphere of being prepared constantly for the opportunity for rescue. Perhaps missing in our culture is a sense of heightened awareness that there are people in need of rescue.

TIM: You know, that's a very interesting thought. Part of the bond that draws into the recovery programs people who have experienced a sense of rescue and a restored hope and dignity, is that they are all in a state of readiness and even feel responsibility to undertake the rescue of others again. Sometimes in such groups there may be a withering of some of that urgency to help the desperately in need. There may be people who feel inadequate or not ready to meet the needs of a person whose feelings are low, who is in bitter despair, in distress and disaster. But the fact that the group has within it people who are willing and able to help, gives power to all persons in the group. As they are part of that group, they share in that readiness as a kind of bond or source of brotherly love and fellowship.

TOM: Could we talk about what can be done to bring more awareness to the confusion so that we can begin to free ourselves from that condition?

TIM: In my own experience, I think that it is to be con-cerned and thoughtful, clearly mindful of others—and that the whole business of self-absorption is that ego tendency that we all have. Being mindful of others is some-thing that I actually attempt to practice during meditation, but also at all times, not just during any one moment. I'm not successful at doing it regularly, but it is a kind of impulse towards others. But I also do not have very often the experience of what others are suffering. I may see homeless people and recognize what they're suffering, but I don't know their full story or inner feelings. I realize that some may prefer not to be bound by the obligations of a conservative society that expects everybody to have a home and a job. I know if I were homeless I would have certain feelings, but I don't know what the conflicting inner experiences of the homeless people actually are. Nonetheless, I need to have some contact with the people who need love, those to whom we can extend some kind of support.

Now love is needed also by the powerful, the oppressors. They are insensitive to the needs of others, the needs of a culture, or the needs of an environment, and may be totally engrossed in the bottom line or whatever else it is that gives them power and focus for their energies. Even though they may have some personal high-minded ethics within themselves, within their families and their social groups, their behavior sounds to me as though it is making a victim of the planet. I know of no way to reach people in that position, to bring into their outlook a willingness to examine their own motives and to transform their own goals towards ones that are more loving. In fact, they may perceive themselves to be very loving. They treat their employees well, they treat their golf partners well, they treat their families well, and they give regularly to charity, so that they may say, "Look, here are all of the reasons and evidences of my being a loving person." But still they may not be aware of what their practices are doing to mankind at large.

I think this attitude is part of the entire American culture. We are the biggest consumers of products on the planet and because of that we are about to go broke. The whole culture fails to recognize the degree to which we are not friends of the planet. So I find it not helpful to focus on just the corporate leaders as the ones who do this. We are all guilty.

TOM: What would you like for yourself with regard to pursuing the question of love?

TIM: I think that love is the greatest spiritual reality— that there is nothing more advanced in the frame of reference of my hopes and takings from life than to be able to love more broadly and more deeply. I regularly ask myself how I may do this, and I find that a good part of how I may do this is to accept other people, other things, all events, death—whatever it is that is there for us to confront, or for us to experience. Until there is acceptance, there's always a barrier between me and any of these other parts of life. That barrier is coming from fear. Fear is what I believe causes almost all of our anti-loving behavior—the fear of deprivation, the fear of loss of something you would prize, the fear of loss of power, prestige, or identity. I find that if I confront the fear, very often the fear is hollow. It's the fear of something unreal, a fear of something I don't have anyway or of losing something that I couldn't lose, or a fear of something that all mankind is going to face, such as death. These fears create a great deal of the self-aggrandizement, the wrong use of individual power, and the acquisitiveness that exists in our world. Therefore, as I confront my fears, I find that I can be accepting of many things that I might not have accepted before. Acceptance is one of the first steps toward love, because I stop being conditional toward others. I don't require that they have certain ways of being; instead I can let them be and accept them. I think that is a loving act.

TOM: Tim, I want to thank you for being here today and talking to us about your life and your perspectives on love. I am deeply honored and appreciative of what you've contributed.

TIM: I'm very grateful to you for this opportunity. I am honored. Thank you.

Postscript

June 24, 1997
Dear Ken and Tom,

When I retired from the position of Public Health Officer at Napa State Hospital I was undertaking a second retirement, having first spent forty years as a professor of medicine at two medical schools in the University of

California system. By the time I left Napa State Hospital in December 1996, I did so with the decision that I would no longer be a professional but purely an amateur. I would make no claim for expertise and be happy to lay aside any mask that might have given me some idea of separation from others, for I found that masks sometimes are used to support false pride.

For a time this decision left me feeling empty and insubstantial, confirming my belief that I had used the mask as support. I then fell back onto the joys of childhood, re-reading what I had read long ago or new works that engaged my interest.

It was especially helpful to meet with friends with whom my wife and I had developed mutual interests, such as in Carl Jung and thinkers who have taken his inspiration in original ways. Jung makes a clean separation between what he can observe objectively and what might be ascribed to his own belief system. He describes the "idea of God" as an aspect of human thought and experience. He objectifies it in his scientific writings, but acknowledged that "I know God" in a television interview shortly before his death. He shows an intellectual rigor and, at the same time, a healing kindliness in his personal and spiritual life as is seen in his memoirs and correspondence. The experience of discussing Jung's ideas and yet going off on one's own under his aura is a help to the amateur standing in which I live and explore.

A feature of Jung's contribution is his attention to the last half of life. He offers a reflective approach to experiences, memories, and dreams free of the probing of a guilty past and childhood injuries, which might help those living in the first half of life to understand and overcome attitudes arising in youth. I find that there is a dimension of the unknown and unknowable within us, and that this dimension is a resource for understanding our sometimes puzzling thoughts and behaviors. The scope of the psyche, as seen by Jung, is so great that there is room in it for the acceptance of death, a concept useful to me in late life. The benefit of age is that while knowing that the past is a rich mine, the present is all: Do not, therefore, let the future spoil this moment.

Sincerely,
TIMOTHY CROCKER

DEE JAEHRLING

Lord,
Make me an instrument of your peace.
Where there is hatred, let me sow love.
Where there is injury, pardon.
Where there is doubt, faith.
Where there is despair, hope.
Where there is darkness, light.
And where there is sadness, joy.

Divine Master,
Grant that I may not so much
seek to be consoled as to console,
to be understood as to understand,
to be loved as to love.

For it is in giving that we receive,
it is in pardon that we are pardoned,
and it is in dying
that we are born to eternal life.

—PRAYER OF SAINT FRANCIS OF ASSISI

DEE JAEHRLING

WAS BORN in South Milwaukee, Wisconsin, on September 14, 1928, the youngest of three children. The Great Depression made finances tight, but whatever we lacked in material goods was made up for by the love and affection of our parents.

I attended Saint Mary's Catholic School and was taught by the Sisters of Saint Francis of Assisi, nuns who gave us not only a sound educational background in our formative years, but impressed us with their kindness. When my brother died of rheumatic fever, the Sisters were a great comfort to my family.

The bombing of Pearl Harbor happened when I was an eighth grader and the shadow of World War II continued through the greater part of my high school years. After graduation from high school, I enrolled at the Extension Division of the University of Wisconsin in Milwaukee. In my second year of college, my parents moved to San Mateo, California, where my sister, brother-in-law, and their two sons where already living.

In 1951, I entered the Order of the Sisters of Saint Francis of Assisi. It was a privilege and honor to come to know and to work with so many beautiful, dedicated people, some of whom were my teachers during my grade school years. I became a teacher and finished college, earning a Master's Degree in Education. I remained a Franciscan for seventeen years, teaching in Chicago, Milwaukee, and Sonoma, California. I left the Order in 1968 and found my way to a work that was dear to my heart, teaching at Hanna Boys Center in Sonoma until my retirement in 1992.

I am enjoying these years of retirement, grateful for each new day which continues to offer opportunities for growth—spiritually, mentally, and socially. I treasure my family and friends and the many blessings and wonderful memories of sixty-eight years.

TOM: Dee, I'd like to welcome you today. It truly is an honor to talk with you as part of our discussions "Elders on Love." Today we want to give you an opportunity to reflect on some issues related to love, community, and spirituality. Is there a way in which you approach the topic of love or think about it or talk about it?

DEE: In reflecting upon my own growth, it's important for me to realize where I learned to love and at what point in my life I recognized the importance of loving another person. I really attribute that to my growing-up years. From the time I can remember I experienced that love in my family with my parents, with relatives, and with my grandmother. I was fortunate enough to grow up in a non-transient era, when neighborhoods stayed neighborhoods and you knew people. Love became almost contagious because you were surrounded with the people you knew. My parents manifested a lot of love for us as we grew up. So modeling was a very important factor. You can't love unless you experience love.

TOM: Do you remember some of the circumstances which were important for your understanding of love?

DEE: Having your parents really give you the understanding that you're important, that the things that you do are important, and the acknowledgment, the awareness that you're around. My parents didn't believe the saying "Little children should be seen and not heard." We could be heard and our opinions were valued.

TOM: Were your parents equal participants in the teaching of love?

DEE: Definitely.

TOM: You talked about neighborhood and the continuity of your neighborhood. How was that also an important ingredient?

DEE: You know the expression "It takes a whole village to raise a child." Well, I experienced that, because if you did something that wasn't appropriate and one of the neighbors would see you, they'd kindly point it out to you. So it wasn't just the parenting, but all the people in the neighborhood that I was exposed to. I'm very grateful for that. I grew up with the same kids throughout grade school and high school. I was taught by Franciscan nuns from first grade to eighth grade, and they were just so loving and kind. When you see that modeled to you and you have that kind of experience . . . it just is important!

TOM: Could you say something about the Franciscan perspective or philosophy on love?

DEE: I was a Franciscan nun for seventeen years. Not only was the modeling present as I was growing up, when I entered the Franciscan community I tried very much to embody the precepts that were taught by the nuns who educated me. I'm very grateful that I was able to teach the youth. I taught in Chicago, I taught in Milwaukee, and then I taught in a school nearby for delinquent boys. At the time when I first started teaching, such boys were referred to as "delinquent." I was not only teaching the children, they were teaching me, and the Franciscan precept was definitely one of love. The prayer of Saint Francis, "Lord, make me an instrument of your peace. Where there is hatred, let me sow love," had deep meaning for all of us in the Franciscan program.

TOM: Do the Franciscans have a particular approach to teaching love?

DEE: When we first entered the convent, we learned that we should manifest what's called "Franciscan joy." If you're joyful, if you experience life around you—and that includes more than people only—then you appreciate nature, you appreciate the environment, and you have a respect for one another. Once you experience the love and the joy, it just becomes a part of you, and joy is as contagious as love.

TOM: Can joy be taught?

DEE: I don't think I could ever teach joy. I could never teach love, but I could manifest it. Love becomes a part of somebody else if you touch them in the right way. But I don't know about teaching it. I couldn't tell you how.

TOM: If you believe that everybody has joy within, what are ways of bringing that forth?

DEE: I was teaching in Chicago, where kids came from the "concrete jungle," so to speak. But there was something about those children—we used to say that it was as if they had grown up in the country. There was something so beautiful about them that we could tell that there must have been a lot of nurturing in their families. Our school was in a very difficult neighborhood. When the public school kids would get out of school or have a day off, they would sometimes do things that weren't very acceptable. One very hot day the window was open when I was teaching fifth grade. One of the boys got up to recite, and through this open window sailed a water balloon and smacked him right on the chest. He was very startled, but the kids just burst out laughing because it was so funny. However, something else could have been thrown through the window, such as a rock. Seeing the joy in a situation that might have been a bit traumatic was something I learned from the kids. "Hey, this isn't traumatic. This is funny." There were many similar incidents in which the children taught me joy and, hopefully, I was able to give it back to them.

TOM: Do you think surrendering to the moment is a critical part of being joyous?

DEE: Exactly. Sometimes you had to forget the lesson plan. "This is the incident. Let's enjoy it. Let's talk about it." As I said, the kids taught me a tremendous amount.

TOM: So perhaps part of the lesson is letting go and enjoying what you have there, instead of following your agenda.

DEE: Recently, I think about two years ago, the community to which I belonged invited all of us who had left to join them for a forty-year celebration of their being in the convent. It was like a forty-year anniversary. They called it a "Jubilee." So I returned and there were former classmates of mine who came from all over the country to join the fourteen remaining in the community. In spite of some very difficult times and hard things that we had dealt with in our community, what came out was how much we enjoyed each other, the humorous things and the beautiful things that we shared, the prayerful life, the walks through the woods. No one talked about the hardships or the negative things that would always happen as you're growing into any phase of life, whether it be religious community, a marriage, or whatever. The joy and the love are what we remembered.

TOM: It sounds like a philosophy for enjoying life.

DEE: Definitely.

TOM: In what way is the Franciscan way different from other spiritualities?

DEE: I think of one word—simplicity. Simplicity is embodied Franciscanism. Saint Francis, of course, was the role model. We took three vows: poverty, chastity, and obedience. Poverty doesn't necessarily mean that you go without three square meals a day; it's what's called the poverty of spirit. Poverty of spirit means that you look to the needs of others. It isn't that you deny yourself the basic needs that you have, but you're very sensitive to the needs of others. Even when we sat down to enjoy a meal together, our Novice Mistress used to say, "Be aware of your neighbors' needs." Anticipate a need. Something as simple as if you are asked to pass the bread, you don't wait to be asked to pass the butter. You did it. So something as little and minor as that becomes translated into larger things. "Be aware of others' needs."

TOM: Could poverty of spirit also mean a deeper clarity of spirit, a sense of being more present to the needs of others?

DEE: Yes, not only to the needs of others, but also being aware of all creation and of simple things. I was fortunate that the convent was located right across from Lake

Michigan. Woods were nearby, and there we would go on frequent walks silently, prayerfully, appreciating the beauty and the change of seasons around us. Just total awareness of all creatures and all of nature, and, certainly, of each other.

I'm not saying people couldn't be difficult at times. Some people weren't very congenial. So we learned how to cope. When I was a very young sister in Chicago, there was a nun who I was absolutely scared to death of because she was so crabby and cantankerous. We had what's called "table reading." At some meals there was silence and then somebody would do some table reading. I mispronounced the word "shrugged"—"He shrugged his shoulders." I don't know if it was a colloquialism where I grew up, but I always pronounced it "shrudged." So this sister grabs me after the table reading and she says, "Don't you know how to pronounce that word?" Then she pointed to the rug and she asked, "What is that on the floor?" I said, "A rug, Sister." So she said, "That's the way you pronounce it." I thought, "Whoa!" One day she was not feeling well. I went to see if there was something that she needed and she said, "No, I don't think so." On the floor was a little carpet. So I said, "Sister, would you like me to shake out your rudge for you?" She burst out laughing, and that taught me humor was the way to get around this sister. Sure enough, from then on, I was okay.

TOM: At that moment, though, you must have trusted that your humor was the right thing.

DEE: Well, it couldn't make things worse.

TOM: It seems like you took a little risk there.

DEE: Could be. Could be. I didn't think about that. It was the first thing that popped into my mind, and from then on I just loved that sister dearly. In such an incident, you become aware of why somebody might be like this—"What is going on?" I was not paying attention to this sister's needs that were making her so cantankerous, and I then found out she was very ill. Her way of dealing with pain was maybe not appropriate, but, again, I learned something.

I had first graders for a while. At the bottom of the steps I had a bulletin board. Around Christmas time there was a caption under it—I don't remember what the caption was—but the first graders couldn't read some of the words. So I happened to be coming down the hallway and the kids were down at the bottom, and one little kid says to another, "What's that say under there?" The other kid says, "I don't know. That's for the people that can't read the pictures." Literally that was true, but I thought, We go through life not being able to read the pictures, the pictures of pain that might not come out appropriately in words. We're hearing the words or reading the words, but we're not reading the pictures.

TOM: Is this the same in terms of relationships, that if we can't read the other person to see what they're going through, if we can't read their picture, then it's a problem sometimes?

DEE: That's true. Not too long ago, oh maybe about ten years ago, my parents were both very ill and I was taking care of them. My mom had had a stroke and she was paralyzed on the left side, but mentally she was still alert. She was quite able to tell about her surroundings, but the paralysis really frightened her. So because of her anxiety, she became quite demanding and not very understanding. That was not her nature, but the stroke did affect her mind in some ways. I had hired some ladies to come in and take care of her while I was teaching at school, and then when I'd come home I was the nurse. The times she'd keep me up all night I was like a zombie, so to speak. One day a friend of mine said, "Dee, is there anything I can do for you? Just ask for anything. The only thing I can't give you is time." You know, time was the only thing I needed. Then some friends came down from Montana to give me time; one would sit with my mother and the other one would get me out of there for a while. To me, that was reading the picture.

TOM: Again there's simplicity to your needs.

DEE: I learned a lot about people from that. They need presence, they need time, and both of these are the manifestations of love.

TOM: You talked about nature being an important aspect of the Franciscan way. Can you say more about that?

DEE: It's a wonderful way to give yourself inner peace. I don't have a huge backyard, but I love it because the birds come in and I enjoy planting flowers. I would get myself together by going outdoors before I entered a classroom. When I taught emotionally disturbed kids for many, many years, it was very important for me to take time for meditation, to go outside and to see the beauties and the wonders of nature. A fragile thing such as a flower or bird just settles yourself and opens your heart to the experiences of the day. On days I couldn't go outside because of oversleeping or some commitment in the morning, I missed that terribly. I realized how important it is to have peace within yourself before you can give it to others, especially to help children. These kids really needed to see that you were okay, that you could see their anger and yet not mirror it. It often happens with us as adults that we mirror the children's anxiety and become anxious. We mirror our children's anger and become angry because of the behavior. If you can mirror peacefulness and calmness, it diffuses so much anger.

TOM: Is mirroring something that we need to look more at as an important aspect of teaching love?

DEE: Oh, I think so. Very many of us often model behavior we do not like. For instance, we see an angry driver in a car on a freeway, and we get angry. So we model inappropriate behavior and it becomes a cycle. You can diffuse anger easily with humor or you can just ignore it. But it's as important to mirror beautiful behavior as it is not to mirror inappropriate behavior.

TOM: You talked a little bit about spirit. What is spirit to you?

DEE: Spirit is joy; spirit is love; spirit is kindness; spirit is many, many things.

TOM: Could we talk about the Franciscan notion of love and community, and how spirit fits in?

DEE: I think spirit is an individual thing. Each one of us has a spirit to manifest that no other human being has. That's why it's so important to recognize your own uniqueness. I saw you recently officiate at a wedding where you manifested such love for the couple. Your face showed the respect and the admiration you had for the entire scene that was taking place, a model for the rest of us to realize its sacredness.

TOM: Thank you. Well, I was involved in a certain ceremony of love. Were there also ceremonies that you were involved in as a Franciscan nun that brought love to the forefront?

DEE: Yes. I remember and treasure the Rubrics, in which we would not only pray with our mind but also with our bodies. So on Rubrics days we would chant out loud and also include bodily movement. One can perform these outward manifestations, but if the mind is not totally present, then it's just movement, it's not praying with your whole being. The Rubrics involved the prayers, the ceremonies of the Mass, and the choir. Anyone who's experienced the music that comes from a convent or a monastery realizes the beauty and the prayerfulness of the songs, and especially the chanting. The days when vows were taken by the nuns who were in training community were extremely beautiful. There were many ceremonies, but those aspects of ceremonies which involved the mind as well as the body were the most important.

TOM: When you're truly present, do you notice that there's a harmony of mind and body?

DEE: Yes, and it's difficult: For instance, you'd ask your-self, "Why am I saying prayers now?"

It's difficult to keep your mind centered and focused because there are so many distractions in our world today, especially with the business and the pace at which our world is moving. We don't have that calm environment.

TOM: I wanted to ask you about the challenges in today's world and what you see as the barriers to loving.

DEE: I think one of the biggest challenges is the lack of time. It's not that we don't have the time. We do not take the time because there are other priorities. We all set up our own priorities. Economics—earning a living—is one of the big priorities. In today's age there are so many man-ufactured needs: We need two cars; we need a television; we need a VCR. All of these cost money, and to pay for them we have to work. Sometimes jobs are at a distance and we've got to commute. Just think of all the hours of the working day that are taken up trying to earn a living! We come home, we're tired. Sometimes there's not the time really to give the quality time that children need. I was very fortunate because we lived in a small community and my father could walk home from work. So he wasn't wiped out when he joined us at the end of the day. There was time for us. I was very grateful for that.

TOM: A number of people realize these barriers to having time, but what do you think people can do to remove them?

DEE: People must realize that they have to pare down a few things in their life and recognize that they need some space to be quiet and to slow down.

TOM: So maybe it gets back to simplicity again. How about for yourself, now? Are there times when you find that you've lost sight of your loving way? What happens at those moments?

DEE: Yes, I would say I get anxious about some things that maybe there's no need to be that anxious about. For instance, sometimes I catch myself not accepting people for who they are, or becoming angry over situations. In fact, just the other day, when I caught myself feeling really angry about someone, I thought, "What's the difference? What's the difference?"

TOM: Could you just say a few things about the different kinds of love?

DEE: Well, obviously, your love for children differs from your love for your parents, and parental love differs from your love for your spouse. My first experience in loving, of course, was what I received from my parents. Then came loving the students that I taught. Some of my students were not very lovable. You find kids who aren't very lovable, but somebody told me, you know, it's the behaviors that you're not loving and that's okay. But the individual is very lovable, and that's not always easy to do. There were times when I would just be happy if so-and-so didn't cross the threshold of the classroom that day. But then you realize how selfish that is.

TOM: It does seem like it's very difficult to make the distinction between unlovable behaviors versus the person.

DEE: That's right. Somebody once said, "You don't have to like someone, but you should love them." It takes a while to understand the difference. But again, as you just said, it boils down to the behaviors. That's what troubles a lot of us. Sometimes what we dislike in others is exactly what we dislike within ourselves. Sometimes the actions of others are mirroring how we behave and that's a lesson in itself. It's important to say, "Hey, I do the same thing," because otherwise it's so easy to judge others.

TOM: What about the love of God or divine love? It seems like that's been a very important part of your life.

DEE: Well, God created us. I remember from my early catechism days, that "We were created in the image and likeness of God." So if we were created in the image and likeness of God, then God is within us. To recognize that God is within me means also that He's within you, He's within everyone we come in contact with. If we keep that in mind, then how can we hate? How can we be abusive? But that's very hard to keep in mind, and it's something we need to bear witness to.

TOM: Was the feeling of divine love something that you've had pretty much all along, or was it something that had to grow in you?

DEE: Oh, it had to grow. Definitely. What my parents gave me was beautiful; they planted the seeds. The nurturing comes from living because your parents aren't always with you. Other people nurture you; your neighbors nurture you. As I said before, the sisters that taught me were nurturing. Nurturing is an ongoing thing. When do you even recognize that it's taking place? I don't know. I couldn't tell you that at one point, "Oh, the light went on that God is within me, that I am manifesting divine love, receiving divine love." There are isolated moments when this would take place. Maybe in childhood. I think when I entered religious life I really did have a strong feeling and recognition about what was happening.

It's like a puzzle. You get the pieces as you go, but you never arrive at the total picture. I know I never will. None of us do because every day adds another dimension to the picture, adds something of the sacred.

TOM: What were some important transitions for you in being able to embody love, share love, or talk about love?

DEE: I think a big transition was the first time I experienced death. I was only six years old when my brother died, and I was very angry. My mother grieved so profoundly that I thought I'd lost her, because she was so focused on having lost her son. I have memories of feeling devastated because not only did I lose my brother, but my mother's gone, too. My sister, who was quite a bit older than I, got my mother out of this and made her realize that "Yes, Bud died, but you still have two other children." Mother recovered from the grief, although when you lose a child, I'm sure you never fully recover. That's the first time I realized how important love was to me.

I don't know when the second transition was or what the progression was, but I know entering the religious community had a profound impact on my prayer life, my realization of who I was, and where I wanted to go.

Another transition which was extremely important was when my parents became ill. When you're a care-giver, something happens to you inside because care-giving takes so much energy, and it's very draining if you don't have help. I remember, after my mother got out of the hospital, a counselor said, "Now, you must be very careful because the statistics say that often a care-giver dies before the one being cared for." I looked at her and thought, "Come on, I can do this." There were times I didn't recognize myself, however. I became very angry at the demands being placed on me—not angry so much at my mother or my father, but angry at the situation. I'd ask myself, "Why is this happening?" and I would get very tired. I'd get extremely impatient. Then I'd have to get myself together and say, "Come on, wait a minute." I'd look at what was happening, and then come back with loving gestures and apologize for my behavior. But that taught me. Before this happened to me, when I'd see people on the street, for instance, shaking a child, almost being abusive, I became angry and I would say, "Oh what's the matter with her or him that they're acting this way?" Now I look at them and say, "What is going on in that person's life that they're manifesting this behavior?" It's so important to experience pain in your own life before you can understand what's behind certain behaviors of other people.

TOM: Developing an appreciation for one's pain and the pain of others seems very important.

DEE: I'm sure some people do not accept it. Again, I have to thank my religious background for giving me the perception, the strength to recognize what was within myself. But there were times when I looked at myself and thought, "You're becoming a demon." I mean, I would go out in the garage and kick boxes, because I was just totally frustrated and sleep-deprived. Oh, that really is a killer. Sleep deprivation can really make you turn into not a very nice person. And that's what was happening to me.

TOM: But I see you as such a caring person.

DEE: You can be a caring person when things are going nice and smoothly. The challenge is when they don't go so smoothly. Even in my teaching days there were students who would exhibit terrible behaviors, and I wasn't always exhibiting being caring about them. I might just blow my stack. Then, afterwards, I'd say to myself, "Oh, wow, you really blew it." But you have to recognize your own human-ness and that these things will happen. You can't always be a loving person, because there's stress that will come in your life and take you off track. The trick is, and the chal-lenge is, recognizing what has just happened, and then getting back on track and apologizing. I had no trouble ever calling a student and saying, "Hey, I blew it, I'm so sorry. I should have recognized you were angry, or you said this, because something's going on. Now, tell me, is there a way I can help with whatever is going on?" Most of the time the student would say, "Oh, that's okay, that's okay." So you're forgiven. It also helps them to realize that by apologizing you're not demeaned, but rather you're enhanced.

I've lived for sixty-seven years now, so I've learned a bit along the way. You don't pick this up at any particular age. You don't learn it by yourself. You learn it from oth-ers that model that kind of loving behavior for you.

TOM: One of the things we're trying to emphasize in this series is communication between the generations. What would you like to see younger generations appreciate or understand? What do you think is missing?

DEE: Well, I think in the family today, the total nucleus is not there. By that I mean we aren't growing up with our grandparents. We aren't growing up with elders because society today is so transient, and sometimes Grandma and Grandpa are miles away or states away. So kids grow up and don't see the needs that the elders have, and the elders miss the grandchildren and don't see the spontaneity of youth. Each generation has a gift to give the other.

My grandmother was the only grandparent of whom I have memories because my maternal grandparents died before I was born and my paternal grandfather died when I was very young. My grandmother lived to be ninety-six, and every year she would come and spend the summers with us. Grandma had a lot of pain. They called it rheumatism in those days—now it's called arthritis. But she was just so wonderful in terms of her engaging me in some of the chores around the house and, even though she was arthritic, she would do these things. Peeling an apple was an experience I'll never forget. Today, if I peel an apple, I think of my grandmother because she always had a story to tell. She taught me respect for a lot of things. We'd go out in the yard and she'd point to a flower or to a blade of grass, and we'd talk about it. So I had the experience of getting these wonderful ideas from an older person, and her gift to me was all the stories and her kindness. I'm sure I also gave a lot to her because of my youth—without knowing it, of course.

But a lot of that is missing today. How many kids are

really with their grandparents? Their grandparents are usually far away; the gap is often because of distance.

I read in our local paper about schools taking children to nursing homes. I think that's one of the most beautiful field trips that a teacher can take their young pupils on. And these nursing home patients just love the kids to death. Sometimes the children will bring their favorite pet such as a hamster or rabbit, and right away there's immediate communication—here's something they can talk about. The kids get a gift from these elder people who show their respect for the youth, and there's laughter as the kids listen to the elders' stories.

Recently, my cousin told me that her seventeen-year-old daughter, Laura, had visited her grandmother. Later, the grandmother called Carol and told her how much she enjoyed Laura's visit. When Carol relayed this message to her daughter, Laura was surprised and replied, "But I was only there for about ten minutes."

TOM: It's just a matter giving someone the time.

DEE: Exactly. And the amount of time isn't the important factor. The thoughtfulness of the visit was the gift to the grandmother. To let Laura know this was a great learning experience for the granddaughter.

TOM: It's a mirroring again. To be able to speak to what we see.

DEE: Laura was made aware that ten minutes of this time is extremely important. So I'm sure she's going to visit her grandmother again and give her fifteen minutes or a half hour because giving is also receiving. And Laura will experience a pleasure doing this because she'll now know how much it means to her grandmother.

TOM: What would you like to communicate or pass on as your legacy to the younger generation about the cultivation of love?

DEE: Appreciate your parents and show your appreciation. Recognize the things that they do for you. Appreciate and value your friendships. It's so important to express yourself, not just in words but in gestures. In summary, I would say appreciate who you are and appreciate your friends and your parents.

TOM: Well, thank you for your tremendous generosity in sharing all of this.

DEE: It's been a pleasure and a great honor, really, a very great honor.

Postscript

February 14, 1997
Dear Ken and Tom,

Over the past few months I have often thought about your project "Elders on Love." I told you at the time of my interview that I felt highly honored that you included me in such an undertaking. The more I thought about it, the more I realized that it was much more than an honor, it was a blessing from the two of you. And now, more than ever, I realize the responsibility such a blessing places on me. Being perceived as a loving person is indeed a compliment. But being perceived that way here is also very humbling. Your project has helped me focus on my own growth in the area of love, helping me realize my abilities in giving love but also my shortcomings in this area. You honored us as elders, men and women who have lived the greater part of our lives. You recognized in all of us something you felt you'd like us to verbalize and share with others. I doubt that any one of us knows exactly what it was that brought us to your attention. But that, for me, is not as important as asking myself what it is I'm doing today about passing on the gifts of love, the blessings I've received from so many others throughout my life.

Ken, I've often heard you refer to these gifts as blessings. I like the word blessing far better than gift because it attaches a meaning that touches on reverence for life. Every time we express love, we bless, we show reverence.

During our group discussion ["Circle of Elders"] we seemed at one time to have gotten caught up in the definition of love. Love can certainly be very complex. And it's certainly not always identified with an easily recognized strong emotion or feeling. But an invitation to express love has a way of nudging us every day, asking us in numerous ways to be kind, to listen, to show concern, respect, tenderness. We meet countless situations where appreciation is welcomed, where expressions of gratitude and gestures of thoughtfulness are immensely appreciated by those receiving these acts of recognition. All too often, I've let the nudges go unnoticed. However, I need to tell you both that since you have gathered seven of us "elders" together, and given us your recognition, I've become much more aware of the countless invitations that occur each day to manifest the precious diamond of love that's been passed on to me by all those who have shown me love, concern, respect. I want to become much more aware and to recognize all the facets of love that beckon for my attention. For awareness is the key!

When I was growing up, there was a little plaque that hung at the bottom of our staircase. Because I passed it so often throughout those years, it's permanently etched in my mind. Since the day that you gathered all of us together I have visualized those words quite often.

> I expect to pass through this world but once. Any good therefore that I can do, or any kindness that I can show, let me do it now; let me not defer or neglect it, for I shall not pass this way again.

I can look back over my life and tell myself I've done some good in this world, I have shown love on many occasions. I can also look back and say that there were many times when I did not express love and concern, when I was not a very loving person. But at this point none of that is as important as the now . . . what about now? "Let me do it now; let me not defer or neglect it, for I shall not pass this way again."

Ken and Tom, thank you for your gift.
Thank you for the blessing!

DEE

JENS HANSEN

Tell a wise person, or else keep silent,
Because the massman will mock it right away.
I praise what is truly alive,
what longs to be burned to death.

In the calm water of the love nights,
where you were begotten, where you have begotten,
a strange feeling comes over you
when you see the silent candle burning.

Now you are no longer caught
in the obsession with darkness,
and a desire for higher love-making
sweeps you upward.

Distance does not make you falter,
now, arriving in magic, flying,
and finally, insane for the light,
you are the butterfly and you are gone.

And so long as you haven't experienced
this: to die and so to grow,
you are only a troubled guest
on the dark earth.

—JOHANN WOLFGANG VON GOETHE
(Translated by Robert Bly)

JENS HANSEN

I WAS BORN in 1924, and with the exception of three years in the Army during World War II, and many trips overseas, I have never lived more than twelve miles from Oakland, California, where I was born. My parents, who had finished college in Europe before they emigrated to the United States from Norway, had five children, of whom I was the fourth and the only boy. My childhood was calm and loving, similar to others of my age whose parents had grown up in the Victorian era.

I married while still at the University of California at Berkeley, and soon had three children and, eventually, three grandchildren. How does one speak briefly about a marriage that lasted forty-eight years? It surely included every human emotion.

I became a very successful architect after a three-year apprenticeship. I am proud of the handsome, eminently livable buildings my firm designed during the thirty-five years that I was in charge of it.

I have pursued years of skiing, auto racing, sailing, and biking, always seeking challenges out of doors. In recent years, I have had great pleasure from my involvement in the men's movement, and the interest in poetry it has brought into my life. In retirement for the past six years, my life continues to be one of great activity and enjoyment.

TOM: Jens, I'd like to welcome you here today. We're trying to find a way to talk about love and to understand what constitutes an awareness of love. Please start with any thoughts you might have.

JENS: First off, Tom, I'm pleased to be here, and to have the opportunity of exploring my thoughts about love.

I've just recently been reading a wonderful book on galaxies. I came away with an understanding that I am smaller than a dot in the cosmos; yet I really feel that we on earth, which is also a dot in the cosmos, are so lucky because we have been given the gift of emotion, and among those emotions is love. At my age, and that of the others that you've been talking to, I've seen a lot of hard times. We all went through the Depression. We saw our parents in great difficulty. We went through World War II, in which forty or fifty million people were killed. Yet, toward the end of our lives, we're still able to experience love. I am madly in love with a beautiful woman. I feel I am one of the luckiest people on earth because of love. Love has hit me so strongly that it gives me such a desire to live for a much longer time.

TOM: What are the feelings that you're experiencing?

JENS: Joy and tenderness and the desire to be with the woman I love overwhelm me. We're currently eight thousand miles apart but we're in constant communication with each other.

Before my wife died two years ago, I was married for forty-eight years. I experienced much love for her, most particularly in the last years of her life when I was taking care of her. A love grew within me and between us that was really incredible. I also have three children and three grandchildren whom I deeply love.

For me the luckiest thing in my life was that I was born to parents who loved each other. I grew up in a very loving family; in my family, being kind to each other was important, caring for each other was natural. I experienced the great love between my parents and among my four sisters and me. I don't think we were encouraged to be loving, that's just the way it was. We were in a situation that was loving.

TOM: What was it about your parents that touched or influenced you?

JENS: Well, I think it was less an education about love than a witnessing of love, being in a family that cared a great deal for each other. There was always a deep closeness among us, which still exists between my sisters and me, even now when we're in our seventies and eighties.

TOM: Could you say more about this witnessing?

JENS: It seems to me that my mother and father were never reluctant to hug and kiss each other in our presence. When my father came home from work, my mother would always meet him at the door and, although she worked very hard during the day, she always made a point of bathing and putting on a clean dress. She always looked nice when she met him. He was always so enthusiastic about hugging her, and they both showed such appreciation for each other.

TOM: So you witnessed very simple things that they would do for themselves and for each other.

JENS: Yes, I think that describes it. There was a kindness, a great kindness and caring for each other.

TOM: At what point in your life did you start to have more awareness of your sensibility of love?

JENS: What I may have thought of as love when I was a teenager was hormone activity. I have a hard time describing love, but it seems to me that it's an extremely intense caring about someone, hopefully with return of the same towards oneself. I have been thinking that it would be hard to be secure in love if you did not have a good deal of security about yourself as well. To be in love, to be intensely in love, to be aware of the intensity of your love would be difficult if you weren't certain that you were lovable yourself. I don't mean you have to be a movie actor or be any super person, but you have to feel that you are worthy, that you yourself are worthy of receiving love. I think you can give love or you can get love, but if you don't give and get love as a pairing of two people, then we're talking about something else.

TOM: I would imagine that there's a certain degree of openness that you need to have.

JENS: I think so. I believe it was Saint Francis who said it is better to love than to be loved, but I don't agree with that. I think to have the maximum out of love, you have to receive it as well as give it. You're both giving and receiving. It's wonderful to give love. I'm thinking of my grandchildren now. I'm so in love with my grandchildren.

They're just beginning to learn what the world is all about, at ages seven, ten, and thirteen. But I understand that they love me a lot. If you, as a mature person, are in love with, and receive love from, another mature person, it's phenomenal, as important as the cosmos.

TOM: Could you talk about mature love, or being a mature person and the sense of love?

JENS: I think it has to do with your whole experience in life, what you feel about life, what you've learned in life. There has to be passion in your life. Maybe I'm quoting somebody, but I think you have to have an ability to feel passion and you have to have great compassion in order to be loved and be lovable. You must have a great sense within your heart of what it means to be a human being in this difficult world. When you have that, it's a most wonderful thing. In the course of my life I have known many people whose main passion was getting money. They may have accumulated a great deal of money, but as far as I'm concerned, it's almost meaningless.

TOM: How is your awareness or consciousness affected when you find yourself in a state of love?

JENS: Well, my consciousness is affected by great joy. I'm excited to hear the voice of my friend, the woman I love. When she telephones me, my spirits rise. When I telephone her and the phone is ringing and I'm hoping she's going to be the one who answers, it's just a thrill. I don't know how to describe it. Wow—it just hits me. That's how I know it.

You often hear that people are attracted to opposites.

That may be true for some persons, but it's been my experience that if you can find someone who is on your wavelength, whose ideals are similar to yours, and whose level of education is similar, you will stand a better chance for a real connection. The woman I am in love with and I are both very interested in our families, our parents, our children, and grandchildren. We're different ages but our family interests parallel each other very closely.

TOM: Are you saying this contributes to a condition of love?

JENS: It contributes to the ability to stay in love. I think prior to love there comes some kind of chemical attraction. I don't know what gets love started. But there seems to be a period of infatuation when you are so attracted to the other person, that their appearance, who they are, what they think, everything about them seems overwhelmingly beautiful and attractive. Now I've been in love for a year and a half and I'm still infatuated with this woman, so it seems to me I've found a rather phenomenal relationship.

TOM: Has there been a deepening of your love?

JENS: We've had some very difficult misunderstandings that came from putting different interpretations on the words that were spoken. On several occasions we've gone through great difficulties. If we hadn't been so in love with each other, it might have been over. Perhaps in love there is a loosening of the ego that allows you to say, "I don't care so much about my own opinion. Maybe my thoughts need inspection and I need to listen to the other person

more carefully and find out what she's feeling." Because
that sentiment was reciprocated, there has been a great
deepening of love during periods of difficulty when we've
come together. It's been like we've come together at a more
intimate level.

TOM: What happened in these moments of misunderstanding and difficult times? What did you notice?

JENS: Oh, I was very angry and I could also recognize
the anger directed at me. It hurt terribly. It hurt to be angry.
I felt self-righteous momentarily, but the thought of losing her was too terrible. Immediately I was busy trying to
recover: "How can I change it?" I think I myself have been
the catalyst for the change. I didn't want to lose the love,
and there was a very receptive party there who didn't want
to lose it either.

TOM: But when you said you were a catalyst—were there
certain steps that you took?

JENS: Well, the first step was to ask myself questions
such as: "What's happening? How can I turn this around?
How can I recover what was there just hours ago? After
months of joy, what caused this to change?" I knew there
had been a misunderstanding. I mentally, intellectually,
calculated how I could reach her again, and asked myself
what actions of mine could cause her to really see who I
was, and who was the person she had loved that now she
apparently didn't love.

TOM: It's interesting, you're talking about using the mind
in some ways to recover this sense of love.

JENS: On one occasion, we had a misunderstanding

about money and it was quite deep and I thought, "I've got to find help. I have to find a path which will lead us to understand each other." In this particular case, I suggested we meet with a very, very good therapist who, in about an hour, was able to bring us back together, to our senses and to our hearts.

TOM: In what way was working with a therapist helpful?

JENS: This therapist knew us both and knew how much in love we were. I think she had difficulty believing that we could not just coast through life together on blue skies. But the therapist is a woman who is very bright and loving and she was able to zero in on both of us, to explain to each of us what our own words and feelings were, and what the emotions were behind our words. And so we could see each other so much more clearly, and we left that hour-and-a-half meeting madly in love again.

TOM: I'm wondering if there is something here we can learn about the use of another person to assist us.

JENS: I think having an outsider is very helpful. Not any outsider, but an intelligent, knowledgeable, compassionate outsider. The lesson may be to loosen up on our attachment to our own ego. Our ego, our love for ourself, our unwillingness to be hurt gets in the way.

TOM: You certainly are someone who has the ability to recognize ego involvement. What could you say about the appearance of the ego?

JENS: Many people, perhaps from an inadequate sense of self-value or self-worth, feel hurt very easily, and as such they are weakened in coming back to compassion or understanding. There is much to be gained if you can just care a little less about being right and care a little more about hearing the other person and paying attention to the meaning of their words. Maybe such an attitude is an extension of compassion.

TOM: Is there a certain amount of honesty in looking at yourself and being able to see in yourself that you're not acting completely sincerely?

JENS: I think it's difficult to see truth if you feel injured. That's where a third party can be really helpful. The third party can assess the relative importance in what's been said.

TOM: Do you think couples get stuck sometimes with respect to their emotional wounds?

JENS: I have many friends who've gotten stuck. I've certainly been stuck myself. In my case, my wife and I used alcohol for relief and that didn't help the love at all. The marriage became a great trial until we were able to overcome the alcoholism.

TOM: How were you and your wife able to work through that experience?

JENS: My wife had great emotional problems from her childhood caused by her father's occupation as a sea captain. He was always leaving the house and going away for months at a time when she was a little girl. So in our marriage she always had a sense that I was going to leave. When the alcohol came along, she let me know that she didn't trust me very much; and once the drinking got heavy enough on both our parts, we got into horrible fights, drunken fights. You hear about marriages in which the couple stays together because of the children. I think such was the case for many, many years in my marriage. But my wife stopped drinking and we gradually simmered down. Maybe it took twelve to fifteen years. I think we loved each other deeply. Maybe by the time I was pushing sixty she began to understand I wasn't going to leave her after all.

TOM: Are there things that you think you can do to nurture love, either in yourself or in your children or friends?

JENS: The best thing to do is to be a kind and generous person. If you can be a decent person and listen to other people, hear what they've got to say, respond to them, you become more attractive to them and they, because they trust you, become more attracted to you. You tend to get a sense of connection. I have a lot of friends, and I think that's the case because we listen to each other and we understand each other. It doesn't mean we have to always be on the same wavelength or have the same things going for us.

TOM: Do you think we can teach this?

JENS: One does it first by example. Teaching morality is hard but I think by example is the greatest way one could do it, by being a decent human being.

TOM: What can we do to create a consciousness of love in the world as a way of assisting with some of the world's problems, and how can we understand what we would need to do to achieve that objective?

JENS: First off you can read the newspaper, you can be

aware of history, and you can understand that even today people live in hatred of each other. Cultures live in hatred and fear of each other. Religions live in hatred of each other. In America religious people live in hatred of other religious people. There must be some understanding that this hatred is self-destructive. You can't hate somebody and be a loving person. You can't love and hate at the same time, because these emotions are so totally opposite. Hatred just blackens your heart. But I sometimes don't have much faith that humans will ever overcome this enormous problem.

TOM: Do you think that love, put into action, truly can be a tool for us to solve some of our global problems?

JENS: I return to the simplicity of being a loving human being, of treating your family in a kind and loving manner, and a hope that this can expand and spread from one person to another, and that we will learn to love and be able to pass love onto the next person. I don't think that the president can say, "Well, let's all love each other." That doesn't work—that's meaningless.

It can't be done superficially. If there can be an understanding that the power of love and being loving can lead to a joyous life as compared to a depressed, hateful type of life, maybe there will be a practical response.

TOM: I'm wondering if we need to move beyond our boundaries of our friendships and our marriages and families to put these experiences, these feelings into action.

JENS: All of us should do what we can. One thing that occurs to me is that there are tools which can make love more intense. I'm thinking specifically of music. Music has been composed that is so beautiful it can open your heart so wide. I feel that I am a loving person and enormously lucky to be so open to love. I get so much response from others that my giving comes back to me tenfold.

TOM: When you find yourself in a state that is not loving, do you take responsibility to try to get yourself back to a loving space?

JENS: I don't like to be depressed. I don't like to be negative. I don't like to be angry. And yet, I experience all of those things. But when they hit me, I embrace them fully, I don't deny them. I just say, "This is not for me, I'm letting go." I am then personally able to become more positive in spite of those negative feelings having gone deeply through me. I can empty my mind of them and become more understanding.

TOM: What other methods do you use to bring yourself into a place of loving?

JENS: Personally, there are my emotions and intelligence, but I also care a great deal about my body. Since I was a child I liked to be physically active and I was always running and jumping. When I grew older I learned how to dance, and I've danced all my life. In the mornings sometimes I'll turn on something exciting on the radio or on my CD; and before I have a cup of coffee, I'll dance for half an hour. I am very conscious of keeping my body in a place that I, and hopefully someone else, might find physically attractive. Clearly, love involves the body and the heart. Love is everything, so it includes everything. I expect that people who don't find themselves loving don't care for themselves physically either.

TOM: So a lack of self-love would be a barrier?

JENS: Yes, I think it would be a big barrier to achieving a beautiful, loving relationship.

TOM: As an elder you have a certain amount of life experience behind you. Is there something you could recommend to the younger generations about being more loving?

JENS: I remember that, when I was a teenager, anybody over twenty-five was a grandfather. It takes a long time. I don't think it's until you're in your forties or even in your fifties that you find that older people are on the same path as you. You find that they haven't gone off someplace where you don't ever want to be. Emotionally, I find myself much more mature than I was in my thirties and forties, much more secure about myself. One thing that helps in whatever you do, whether it's finding love or succeeding in your professional pursuit, is keeping a really open mind. If you can listen and be in a place where you're not responding in your head while you are listening, I think you're going to hear a lot more than you normally would. You're going to learn a lot more.

TOM: Do you think you can challenge yourself to remain more open?

JENS: That's a very good way to put it. Really challenge yourself to keep a wide open mind. Also, I don't think you can look for love. I think love happens.

TOM: It's something that arises more out of the moment?

JENS: Yes, I think it arises out of the moment.

Also, I've known a lot of women who are turned off by men who exhibit great neediness. It's probably true of men towards women, also. But you have to be accepting and open to whatever comes along. I don't think you can say, "I'm going here or there to find someone to love."

We haven't talked about sexuality in all of this but I think that's a big part of the advantage of being in love. When you're in love, sexuality or sex becomes ten times more enjoyable. Sex has always been good for me, but when you're in love, it gets heightened to levels that you never would have reached if there wasn't a loving relationship at the same time.

TOM: Can you say some more about that? What have you noticed?

JENS: My experience is that men are more needy than women, more sexually active, more desirous of sex. This neediness can get in the way of finding love. A calmer approach, getting to know the other person, really becoming a friend before entertaining sex in your life, may be a wiser way to go. It's very difficult. It is well known that generally men need sex in order to find love, and women need love in order to achieve full sexual satisfaction. But when you get older, you calm down. Maybe the lessening of the hormone activity has something to do with it. Yet I don't feel I've lost a thing . . . I enjoy my sexuality now perhaps more deeply than I ever did before.

TOM: Looking forward now, what would you like for yourself? What are you still yearning for?

JENS: Well, in my case, I have prostate cancer, which

I've had for over six years. Fortunately it is very slow growing. So I yearn for a long, long life. I'm seventy-two and
I'd like to be about ninety-two before I go. But I figure I
have another four or five years or more and I intend to be
as emotionally and intellectually conscious as possible during those years. With the help of Alcoholics Anonymous,
I have quit drinking for two years, and it's been a blessing
for me to have been able to do that. I really enjoy waking
up in the morning and making my plans for the day:
Whom will I see? Whom will I phone? Whom will I talk
with? What will I read? What will I listen to? This after-
noon I'm going to watch my ten-year-old granddaughter
go horseback riding. That's exciting. I love to be alive.

TOM: When you see other members of your generation,
what do you admire, thinking, "I'd like to have a little bit more
of this quality in my own life"?

JENS: I feel very rewarded with my life. I really admire
couples who have been together for a long, long time and
who have achieved a close, intimate relationship. I respect
those who've really solved the issues of intimacy and understanding and have remained in love. I think that's such
a fantastic thing and it clearly takes effort. I think you have
to learn how to let your ego relax, because of the many
things in life that challenge you. You have to hear the challenge and let go in order to keep yourself open and
available.

TOM: Can we learn to observe the ego in action?

JENS: Yes, I think it's possible to be aware of your reactions as they happen. When you have this awareness,

you can modify your actions as they are occurring. It also helps to observe others who have been able to do it, and by witnessing people who are very secure in life and are achieving many delights out of being alive.

In addition to the book on the galaxies that I referred to earlier, I've been reading a book with text and many pictures of World War II. I think we have to be very careful not to be conned by charismatic people. How civilization could have come that far and yet have the whole world go to war is difficult to understand—almost incomprehensible. I think you have to be very, very aware of what people are saying and compare it with their actions.

TOM: Do you think that in some ways we're being conned now?

JENS: I think great efforts are being made to destroy education. There is a growing development of a very small elite in the world who will govern the rest of us. The majority will be entertained by games—football, basketball, baseball—drugs, and alcohol. However, there are people with a similar sense of this trend who are willing to fight it, who are willing to sacrifice and to teach and to reach out and try to prevent it from happening. In this gigantic never-to-be-understood cosmos, here on this little spot called earth, a relatively short time ago life was created with the potential for great intelligence and great love. What more could one ask for than brains and a heart? It's the miracle of miracles that we exist and we must all work to make this the paradise it has the potential of becoming.

TOM: Maybe we have a lot to learn about the use of intelligence and love, that we still need to have discussions like this to understand how to master these areas.

JENS: I think there are parts of society that didn't exist fifty years ago just coming to an understanding of what the issues are. But the forces of good and the forces of evil are both human forces. The forces of good have really got to organize and develop tools to educate. Love is one of the tools that hasn't been recognized enough as of this date because we've been relying on our minds to solve the problems. If we can open our hearts and educate others to open their hearts, there may be some hope to it all.

TOM: As an elder, do you feel you have a role in educating the younger generation about the lack of hope and the misguided directions that people are taking?

JENS: Well, you mentioned the younger generation. That's clearly where my interest is because of my grandchildren. I cannot contemplate them growing up in a hopeless world. I want them to grow up being offered everything that I've been offered and more. And I really try to stress how much I love them, so that when they're in their thirties and forties, they can look back and say, "Wow, my grandfather really loved me," and they would understand how important love has been in their life.

TOM: You're saying that love is one gift that you can give your grandchildren.

JENS: Absolutely, and there's plenty of love to give. There's no limit to the amount of love that's available. The more you give, the more you get. It's so exciting to love and to be loved; nothing beats it. And there's absolutely no reason to hold back. If you feel some compassion or passion or love, don't keep it to yourself, let it be known, pass it around.

TOM: It's an interesting paradox. But if someone is not feeling hopeful, maybe it's difficult to be loving.

JENS: I can't answer that one except to say, "Keep on trying."

TOM: Part of the message might be that you have to work to move beyond hopelessness.

JENS: Perhaps when you're in despair, you need to know that help is available, or at least that there's tomorrow and tomorrow you may be feeling differently, or maybe you will find some answers—that being stuck in a place is not forever.

But it does require personal effort. You can't expect it to only come from outside. You have to open yourself up to it as well and to start acting. If you act in a loving way, then circumstances can become loving. Acting in anger can quickly turn to real anger. If you are kind and generous, you're going to get rewards that may turn into love.

TOM: You mentioned that there truly is an abundance of love in the world. Yet I think that there is an enormous withholding of love, either individually or collectively, in our world now.

JENS: It occurs to me that the expression of love is often withheld because one is afraid that it will be misunderstood or ignored or derided; there is a fear of non-acceptance by the other party. However, when you express love or express caring, almost always it's really welcomed. The point I want to make, which has to do not only with love but with kindness and generosity of spirit, is that the expression of love is so important that one has to be brave! I often tell younger friends of mine, "Take a chance. Tell somebody of your love. Don't miss an opportunity to express love. Maybe you won't see that person again, but expressing that love could really influence both your lives for a long, long time. Be brave, take a chance. Tell somebody of your love."

TOM: This is a very straightforward and excellent recommendation. To put love into action we need to take the chance, to show some courage and reach out.

JENS: The obverse occurs to me right now. If somebody says "I love you" or expresses love or is kind to you, receive it! Don't be suspicious of love. Just accept it and see what happens. Be brave and take a chance, both in giving love and receiving it.

Postscript

February 28, 1997
Dear Ken and Tom,

In the months following our wonderful group meeting, I have often thought about the many views that were shared that day. In spite of the gentleness of the get-together, I find that it was a very provocative meeting. It has caused me to think a lot about my life and my relationships to others.

Over the years of my life I have moved from being a "true believer" to becoming an atheist. When I gaze at the sky on a clear dark evening with the knowledge that the stunningly beautiful millions of stars I see are but a microscopic fraction of our own galaxy, and that the universe is made up of billions of galaxies, each with billions of stars, I am happy to accept the American Indian philosophy that I am part of the "Great Mystery." That is okay with me and enough for me.

In recent years, I have come to understand that our lives are largely determined by circumstances, most particularly by the issues of where we are born and to whom we are born—in other words, our environmental experience and our genetic heritage. The details of our lives and the twisting paths they follow seem to be decided by "fate," by unplanned coincidence.

I am in love with a beautiful woman who lives in Argentina, 8,500 miles from my home. We write, telephone, and see one another regularly on long visits to each other's countries. We are developing a close relationship such as I have never experienced before. Was it coincidence that we both should meet at a workshop, she traveling from such a great distance, and me, several months after my wife's death, away from my home for the first time?

Our meeting can be considered a coincidence, certainly a happy one. But I think, in fact, it occurred because we had both developed, with great determination and effort, an open mind and an open heart.

My thinking in these past months has reinforced my opinion, expressed in the interview, that with conscious effort we can free ourselves from those traits of our personality which lead to rudeness, avarice, cynicism, hatred, and indifference—surely a description of depression. With conscious effort, courage, and help from others we can cultivate feelings and actions of courtesy, kindness, generosity, and compassion. The rewards are great: friendship, joy, energy, and life. And who knows, with the right coincidence, maybe love!

Love to you both, from
JENS

ELIZABETH LÉONIE SIMPSON
& JOHN WURR

Let there be spaces in your togetherness,
And let the winds of heaven dance between you.
Love one another but make not a bond of love:
Let it rather be a moving sea between the shores
of your souls.
Fill each other's cup but drink not from one cup.
Give one another of your bread but eat not
of the same loaf.
Sing and dance together and be joyous,
but let each one of you be alone,
Even as the strings of a lute are alone though
they quiver with the same music.
Give your hearts, but not in each others' keeping.
For only the hand of life can contain your hearts.
And stand together, yet not too near together:
For the pillars of the temple stand apart,
And the oak tree and the cypress grow
not in each others' shadow.

—KAHLIL GIBRAN

ELIZABETH LÉONIE SIMPSON

I WAS BORN in Pasadena, California in 1928, the fourth daughter of the paleontologist George Gaylord Simpson and step-mother psychologist Anne Roe. I grew up in Washington D.C. and New York City. I attended Tufts University and the University of Michigan from which I received degrees both in English and Spanish Language and Literature, as well as a master of arts degree in Linguistics.

During the midfifties, as a single parent with three children, I returned to California, taught Spanish in high school, and later joined Harcourt Brace Jovanovich as editor of a new social science series. That position evolved into a contract as co-author which financed my enrollment in a doctoral program at the University of California at Berkeley. After graduation, I took a post at the University of Southern California where I was also able to complete a postdoctoral year of work in developmental psychology.

Several years of strenuous consulting followed and, possibly as a result of exhaustion, I developed tubercular meningitis which devastated my capacity to remember so badly that, for some time, I could neither read or write. After a prolonged recovery, I returned to my career in academia, teaching, and writing. Altogether I have authored or co-authored fourteen books of fiction and nonfiction.

In 1996 I retired from the California School of Professional Psychology, but I am continuing to write mythic fiction, poetry, and a nonfiction work on social and personal memory. I live in the Santa Cruz mountains with my husband, John Wurr, a Golden Retriever, and a gray cat—all beloved!

JOHN WURR

I WAS BORN in London in 1925. I remember a wonderfully happy childhood as a member of an extended family. At ten years of age I left home to become a boarder at Highgate School in London. The school was fairly close to home and, until the outbreak of World War II, I came home each weekend. At the beginning of the war, the school was evacuated to Devonshire where we spent four rather hungry but physically energetic years enjoying the ocean and the open countryside.

From school I went directly into the army and soon found myself in Italy as a signaler providing close air support for the Eighth Army. After three years in Italy and Austria, I was demobilized and went, with the British equivalent of the G.I. Bill, to Oxford University where I "read" (majored in) physics. After taking a graduate degree in Electronics at London University, I came to California with my wife and young family, intending to stay only two years. Five years later, I joined a spin-off from Litton Industries founded by some of my former colleagues and remained with that company until my retirement twenty-seven years later. I found my job—engineering the production of microwave vacuum tubes—fascinating because of the constant challenge of problems to solve.

In 1980, I re-met Elizabeth Léonie Simpson, with whom I had become friends seven years earlier at the Sunnyvale Unitarian Fellowship. We were married in 1981 —presenting Elizabeth with six more children, three of whom were still living at home with me.

Retirement is not the easy, relaxed life that I had expected. With a home with five-and-a-half woodland acres to maintain, an apartment house in San Jose to oversee, a Golden Retriever to exercise, theater, symphony, and travel, there is never enough time.

TOM: Elizabeth and John, I want to welcome you here to this discussion on what elders feel about love. We're attempting something fairly ambitious, which is to find a way to talk about love and, in some ways, to relate it to the topics of spirituality, community, and communication between the generations. Where do you think we should begin today to talk about love? Where would you like to begin?

ELIZABETH: I think I would feel most comfortable if we started with the definition of love. This may sound a little strange, but when John and I started to talk about this recently we found ourselves somewhat confused, and perhaps a little troubled, by the fact that there are so many definitions of love. One is compassion, one is sexual or romantic, one is something that could just be called caring for people. Another definition is the one I suspect we elders are most concerned with, and that is relationship love: the love that is built on trust and respect and gratitude.

TOM: You mention "compassion"—a word that has come up in some of our other discussions. For you, how does compassion relate to the theme of love?

ELIZABETH: I think that as one gets older, one becomes more aware—particularly in an age of greatly enhanced communication—of the needs of other people around the world. One can deal with that awareness either by closing it off and ignoring it or by contributing more because of a greater sensibility about those needs.

TOM: Do you think that, in our society, we've attained much collective compassion? Do we have more compassion now than previously?

ELIZABETH: I think it is very difficult to say whether this is so, for when one hears members of Congress say over and over again: "It's not in our national interest," one worries that it's compassion that is falling by the wayside.

TOM: What do you think they are trying to convey by referring to "national interest"?

ELIZABETH: I think it has more to do with domestic economics and political safety than it has to do with the needs of all the peoples of this world.

TOM: John, what do you think about compassion in the world?

JOHN: I am optimistic that the world is becoming more compassionate. I realize that there may be difficulty in believing this when one remembers the Holocaust or the recent events in Bosnia and Rwanda. However, one of the reasons that we are more compassionate is that we know about what is going on in the most distant parts of the world. When I was a boy, in the thirties, if thousands died in India from famine we barely knew of it. At the most, we saw a small paragraph in the better newspapers. Today such events are brought right into our living rooms and people can't help but respond. Things certainly aren't as good as they should be but, in some respects, I believe there has been an advance. Until World War II, war was still an acceptable policy for a number of the Western industrialized countries. I don't believe that any of them now believe that it's a feasible option. You might say that events in Bosnia and Herzegovina have gone to excess, but even in this instance, the conscience of the world forced us to intervene. We also take immediate steps to do what we can to alleviate starvation and disease in distant countries. That would not have happened in the 1930s. Of course, there was no United Nations then, but also there wasn't the will and, weak as that will may be, I think it is growing stronger.

ELIZABETH: I want to go back for a minute to what John said. It seems to me, if I remember my mythology correctly, that Venus is married to Mars, so there is an interesting juxtaposition of love and war. Maybe in some ways it's the dramatic situations that elicit a type of compassion and love and caring. That's perhaps why, in mythology, Mars and Venus are mates.

TOM: So you are saying that an atmosphere of opposites is necessary?

ELIZABETH: Perhaps. I suggest it might be so and that's why they are linked in mythology.

TOM: You are the only couple with whom we will be speaking in our discussions. Have you two talked about love and your relationship?

ELIZABETH: Very much so. There was an interesting couple of days in our lives when we sat down and really tried to analyze, not just our relationship, but the meanings of love in the broad sense. We discussed our beliefs about relationships in both personal and social terms.

TOM: What are some of the things that came to mind?

JOHN: First of all, we divided love into four categories. There may be more categories, but we both agreed that real love is mature love. We've talked about compassion—

that's one form of love. We've talked about romantic love very briefly which is a fantasy that most young men and women have—and it's very exciting. But that intensity isn't going to last. I remember how much I enjoyed the giddy fantasies of infatuation when I was young, but I think I always knew that these were not real love. You asked whether my idea of love had changed. I think I always knew what I considered love should be and I believe that was because I felt it so strongly with my parents. I thought when all this great excitement is over—and it's absolutely marvelous while it lasts—I want it to mature into this thing which I consider real love. My mind hasn't changed on that.

When I married Elizabeth—my second wife—I said, "You're the person I want to marry, but I probably won't love you for many years." I didn't say this to my first wife, but I knew it. My first wife and I were wildly attracted to each other and this was great. But I've always felt that the real thing, real love, the permanent thing, has to grow slowly and is based on helping, struggling, and succeeding together. This is what I think love is and this is certainly what has happened with Elizabeth and me over a period of time.

TOM: Sounds like you knew you were in a new phase of life, that you were making a passage from a previous type of loving to a more mature love together.

JOHN: No. You misunderstood slightly. Even in my first marriage I said, "This is wild, this infatuation we have, this great passion we have for one another—but I don't believe it is reasonable to expect that it will last." I always had in mind that it had to develop into feelings such as those I had for my parents (and a very few others)—feelings of complete trust and the certainty of knowing that they would be there for me at all times. I expected that this would happen in my first marriage and it did happen. But when I married Elizabeth, I said to her, "You know that it is going to take a few years for this to come about. It can't happen overnight."

ELIZABETH: Part of this is the fact that John's relationship with his parents, especially with his mother, was based on a set of expectations. It wasn't simply unconditional.

TOM: What was your response when he said this to you?

ELIZABETH: John's not talking about unconditional love—which I absolutely do not accept as possible. Because of John's deep feelings for his parents, and particularly for his mother, there were certain things that he knew she expected of him. She expected him to be lovable, but, because he was a particular type of person, she would never have to say, "Well, you did this and I don't love you any more!" That would never, never, have occurred. But, nonetheless, he knew what she expected him to be and the love was based on his succeeding in being that person. He and his mother defined each other as decent, lovable persons.

TOM: So right from the start of your marriage you had some discussion about what love meant to each of you.

ELIZABETH: Oh, we had discussions about his mother and the fact that he was one of the very few lucky people in this world. He had a mother who was a healthy human being and who loved him—as his father did, too—but she was even more able to convey that love in a very healthy way.

TOM: John, would your parents talk about love as a way of trying to raise or educate you? Or was it more by example?

JOHN: It was by example. I don't remember any discussion about this.

TOM: So it was more an atmosphere of love in the home, and the level of caring that your parents showed.

JOHN: I was also fortunate in living in a very warm extended family. Not only my parents, but my aunts and uncles were all happily married and we saw a lot of them and our cousins. And there were other examples, too, particularly my godparents who obviously loved each other deeply. Examples such as these showed me what love was and this is what I aspired to. So the crazy giddiness I went through when I was infatuated was delightful, but I felt that it wasn't the real thing.

ELIZABETH: My experience was different: I went away to college at seventeen, to Tufts College, as it was called then (it's now University), and for me, it was freedom! Absolute freedom for the first time. Within a couple of months I met a young man who had just returned from service in the Navy. He was twenty-five years old and I fell madly in love. He reciprocated, but I don't think I had the maturity or wisdom to know that, if this relationship was going to endure, it would have to be based on the qualities that John's talking about. I was a romantic; I had an idea of love which probably could not endure. I am embarrassed to say that, although I think I'm a much more mature person now, there is still an element of the romantic in me. I like the—what shall I say?—decorations of love which ornament a very solid base of trust.

TOM: What are some of the challenges for couples who begin romantically and then endure through the changes of love over the years?

ELIZABETH: One thing we both solidly agree on is that the current practice of living together before marriage is a very good idea. Then you see people in everyday situations and you respond to each other's reactions. You learn to know each other in ways that, in the past, couples didn't until after they were married. The possibility of error when you haven't had a trial period is just enormous. So that's a change that seems to be for the better.

TOM: It's a way of being more informed about who a person is and maybe making better judgments about commitment.

ELIZABETH: One of the things I am very much aware of—and I'm sure John is, too—is that, as you become older, neither has his or her own way. A successful love is based, first of all, on an awareness of the other person and, second, on a willingness to respond to that awareness. When my husband says to me—I have to laugh when I tell you this—"I don't want the window open when we go to bed at night," I say to him at first, "Why? Do you want to sleep in a stuffy room?" But if he feels strongly about it, then I don't open the window. It's a very small compromise but it's typical of the kind of very small compromises that go on during a relationship.

TOM: What do you see as some of the barriers that people face in experiencing love, manifesting love, or expressing it?

ELIZABETH: Well, the first and very obvious one goes back to the famous saying of the Delphic Oracle, "Know Thyself." If you don't know the things that are primary in your life, or the way you wish to live your life, or your own personality, you can't know whether or not you and the person you love can fulfill these needs together. John and I have discussed this very much indeed. One has to have a belief in one's own capacity to love and one's own worthiness to be loved.

TOM: Can we say to younger generations, "These are important values," or are they just something you have to learn by yourself?

JOHN: I don't know whether we can teach these values, but it's worth a try. I really think that having a successful long-term relationship is a great challenge and, if you succeed, then you should regard it as a major accomplishment for you as a human being. I think that if you have self-esteem and pride, that is, that if you believe yourself to be a lovable person, you would expect to be able to achieve this. I know that, if you do have a long-term successful relationship, you have every reason to be proud of yourself and your partner. I believe what the Church of England prayer book says about marriage: that it should be "for richer or poorer, through sickness and in health." Every marriage has its ups and downs and it requires grit and perseverance to succeed. What you must not do is say, "Well, I'll try someone else. This person is so troublesome, I'll look for someone else." That is very foolish because real love is forged in the fires of pain and difficulty.

ELIZABETH: Or maybe you can say that it is forged by pain and difficulty which is transcended by cooperation between the two.

JOHN: Yes, I do mean that. If you stick together in difficult times, I think you can look back and feel proud of one another. I don't want to be political about this, but I feel warmly towards Bill and Hillary Clinton because they have had difficult times but they have stuck together. I respect both of them for it.

TOM: What you are saying is very powerful because, when you think about the divorce rate in our society, a lot of people don't have the faith that perseverance is what's needed. Can we communicate to people that out of this perseverance there may be hope for saving a relationship?

ELIZABETH: I think people are marrying older, and though I would be the last to say that age necessarily brings wisdom, it does bring experience. When I first married, I was twenty years old. I didn't know myself and I didn't know my partner, really. We both believed that it would be a lifelong relationship, but there wasn't any reason to believe that. I didn't realize that we would both evolve over time—and in different ways.

TOM: But when the two of you met, was there something that you recognized in each other? Was it love?

ELIZABETH: We have to laugh a little about that be-cause when John and I first met we were both happily married—to other people. We were members of the Unitarian Fellowship in Sunnyvale, California. We became friends, just friends. My marriage ended and we kept in touch with letters once a year as I went back to school in Berkeley, and to the University of Southern California where I took a professional post. Later I moved up north to Berkeley. Then I got a Christmas card from John telling me that his marriage had broken up and how busy he was. I might as well tell you the rest of the story. I wrote him back a postcard which I think he will never forget be-cause he tells the story to everyone. It just said "Promises, promises, promises" with a telephone number on it.

JOHN: I'm sorry to do this, but it's a husband's duty. [Both laugh.] She really wrecked that story. We used to send each other Christmas cards. I sent her a Christmas card one year and said that my marriage had broken up. She sent me a card back, saying, "I am now living in Berkeley. Come up and see me." I didn't go because I was left with my three boys and I was so busy trying to do all those things that single working mothers have to do. You know, shopping, cleaning, cooking, et cetera. But a year later when I looked over my previous year's cards I found the one from Elizabeth which said, "I'm living in Berkeley now. Why don't you come and see me?" I send her an-other Christmas card with the message, "I'll come up and see you some time." By return mail I received a plain white card which said "Promises, promises, promises" followed by a phone number and signed "Elizabeth." So I picked up the phone and talked to her and then visited her the next weekend. And by probably the third weekend I had decided this was someone with whom I felt extremely comfortable. So I said, "Come down and live with me [in Sunnyvale] because I can't be away from my boys so much." When she said, teasing, "But I like living here because the condominium has such a nice swimming pool," I said, "I have a nice swimming pool, too." So she came and after a year of continuing to get on very well, I asked, without any pushing from her, "Would you marry me?"— and that was it.

ELIZABETH: And we have been married for fifteen years this week. So it's a good long time, far longer than my previous record, and it will endure for the rest of our lives; we both know that.

TOM: That's wonderful! So it started off as a friendship and it evolved?

ELIZABETH: Yes, it did. I was teaching at the time we became acquainted and because I wanted to upgrade my salary, I had to take another course. So I took a course in existentialism. My husband wasn't interested in that but John was, so he drove me to the college each week. He took the course as well, not for credit but just for interest. We had good talks going there and back and really got to know each other, but there was nothing sexual about it in the slightest. It was just that we were attracted as good friends. When he came back into my life, I think it was a recognition of that—of our being good friends.

TOM: You mentioned having a common interest. The

mutual interest in existentialism seemed to have been important for your sense of connection.

ELIZABETH: Well, just being Unitarians did that for the two of us, although we've argued about that. We have slightly different definitions of what the church means to each person who belongs. But that's all right.

TOM: Is there something about your shared interest or involvement in the Unitarian Church that relates to this theme of love?

ELIZABETH: Well, I think that's so in the sense of what one could call circumscribed or controlled freedom, the freedom to believe, which I think is also part of an appropriate loving. Each person has to have the freedom to believe in certain ways and the freedom to do certain things within those bounds. The constraining boundary comes from the need not to hurt other people.

TOM: You're bringing something very important into the discussion, about pairing freedom and love. How do you see freedom as being important for a healthy relationship?

ELIZABETH: When we started talking about this and writing it down a bit, we decided that freedom is terribly important, but that it absolutely has to be defined by the person him- or herself. It can't be something that is constrained by someone outside, and it certainly has to include an awareness of the needs of the other partner. So it's still freedom all right, but modified by this awareness, an awareness that is part of love. There is no doubt about that. The willingness to respond to the knowledge that something might hurt someone or that they might be troubled by some action is certainly part of the loving process, at least in this definition of love.

JOHN: I think that total freedom is as incompatible with marriage as it is with a civilized society. You can't have total freedom because it would hurt other members of the society. If you love someone, you don't want to hurt them. Therefore, you don't do things that would hurt. Now, it is very important that this discipline comes from within and that you yourself control the limits of the things you do because you don't want to hurt the other partner, because you value the other partner and you want them to stay and to be happy. But, at the same time, you must never have a lurking feeling in the back of your mind that this is being forced upon you by the other. You must know that you are doing it because you care about the other person and because you want them and value them.

TOM: Is this something the two of you have had all along or has it evolved?

ELIZABETH: I think from what John says—and I'm willing to believe him—that he knew this much earlier than I did. Sometimes I think that this marriage is probably the one I should have had when I was younger. Except that I was too young and flighty to have had it then. I think that, at that time, John was more mature than I was. I didn't know many of these things until later on. There are aspects of love between people who are going to live together and share their lives that need learning: granting privacy, not dumping on the person, not telling it all. I realize that

I am going against a very broad, popular psychological belief that "dumping" is useful. And I think that it is, under some circumstances, but in a close relationship it can be threatening and destructive. I think of Sid Jourard, a well-known clinical psychologist, who used to talk about "the transparent self" and the need for being clear, being and admitting what you are very publicly, even admitting some socially negative qualities. But when one looks at Jourard's writings, as well as his life—he was successfully married and had three sons—you found that he very much modified this belief over a period of time. You see, he also talked about the need for privacy. He talked about the fact that some things cannot be shared because, just as John has said, they would not be useful in building a relationship that is going to endure. You keep some things to yourself out of love.

TOM: I think a lot of couples struggle with this very issue about how honest or direct to be with one another. That is, should one be totally forthright with one's feelings and observations or should one protect one's spouse?

ELIZABETH: Of course, one has to add to that, it depends on what you're doing. If you're a cheat and not telling, that's a very different matter. But if you are simply keeping some aspects of your feelings or doings in the past to yourself, that may be very useful. In fact, more than useful, very important.

JOHN: In our relationship I think that we are both closer to one another than to any other person. If I have problems, Elizabeth is the one I want to share them with first. Mind you, I wouldn't want to dump on her. One can share problems in a loving way or in a hurtful way.

ELIZABETH: I think that's true. I didn't mean to minimize what you said there because I do think that some things happen within relationships that, if you just bury them, they will fester forever. To be able to bring them to the surface and to discuss them is terribly important.

TOM: Is this a skill we can teach or, again, is it something that has to be learned through tough experience?

ELIZABETH: Well, I think that it can be taught through role models, but with great caution. I taught counseling at the University of Victoria in British Columbia for a while, and it was easy for me to see that, in teaching a course like that, you can put into your students' minds some ways of behaving that might never have occurred to them. One of these ways is openness, a willingness to discuss what is troubling you and not do it in an attacking way. Another way is simply to know where the weight, the bulk, of the problem belongs. One useful capacity is simply to be able to say, "That's someone else's emotional problem and not mine." Putting such knowledge to work can be an act of self-preservation.

TOM: That's interesting to me because I think we're moving into an era of skepticism about the value of counseling and psychotherapy. Do you see counseling as an arena in which we can talk about love or teach people about love?

ELIZABETH: I think it can be extremely useful, but it depends upon what you mean by "counseling." I'm not a therapist, I'm a developmental psychologist and have never been trained to be a psychological clinician. So I want to make very clear that I speak as an outsider here. But it seems to me that the first thing that someone in need of emotional help needs to know is that there is a great range of theory and philosophy underpinning the therapy that is available. Someone in need of help should look until he or she finds the right person. That person may be an eclectic, someone who draws from a lot of different sources. Or that therapist may be a straight-line post-Freudian, a Gestalt theorist like Fritz Perls, or one like Abraham Maslow, who is a contemporary of humanistic psychologists such as Jim Bugental. You have to find someone who can respond to your needs and your temperament, so you won't be wounded in the process, so you'll be healed.

JOHN: Psychology is not my professional field, but it seems highly probable that you could teach this sort of thing if you can teach diplomacy, that you could probably teach people how to deal successfully with other people, including the ones they are going to love. At lunch time we were talking about Jimmy Carter and his great success at mediating. He seems to have the ability to go in there and diffuse situations. But isn't this a form of what is called "conflict resolution"?

ELIZABETH: Yes, it is. There's a lot of that being done today. And you have to be neutral to teach conflict resolution; you have to be a person who isn't emotionally involved in what you are teaching.

JOHN: I'm not just talking about the practical mediation between couples who have problems. I'm saying there must be general principles—how you approach things. For instance, you don't approach things aggressively. You turn the question. You explain the point of view of the other party, such as, "Now I just talked to so-and-so and he feels that he can't possibly give up that land on the Golan Heights because of so forth and so on." I think it would be a very worthwhile thing to do. As far as teaching it in school, I think it could be taught in high school, if you like.

TOM: I think it's remarkable that California, as a state, has taken on this task of trying to foster, or promote, self-esteem. Does this in some way relate to loving?

ELIZABETH: Yes, John Vasconcellos, a California Assemblyman and now State Senator, has made a cause of promoting self-esteem. A lot of fun has been made of this as a superficial thing. The fact is that genuine self-esteem is based on real achievement, and not just saying, "I love myself; I am a good person; I am of value." That is useless. Genuine self-esteem must be based on the awareness that you do have value—to yourself and to others. One of the real problems today is unloved children—children who, right from the start, are not valued by a parent or caretaker, someone who truly loves them and shows them that they are wanted and important.

TOM: What do you think we can do about unloved children?

ELIZABETH: It is an extremely difficult problem. There's no question about it. One of the things that increases the difficulty is what goes on in the political arena. Monies get cut for counseling in school; monies get cut for training clinical psychologists; monies get cut for services for the poor. It is very, very hard for many adults, who are trying to make a living, to have the emotional or physical energy to be loving to children when they are struggling to stay alive.

JOHN: I think it goes back to when you're a child. You have to have some model of what you consider a good person, so that you can recognize clearly what the qualities of a good person are. If those qualities are imbued in you thoroughly when you are a child, when you slip from them you will lose self-respect. If you meet your ideal of what a good person is, you gain self-respect. As Elizabeth remarked, you can't just say, "I'm a good person." You must have a model of a good person to say, "I'm a good person, I feel like I'm a good person because I am like the person whom I respect." So these ideal qualities have to be taught and I don't think that it is impossible to do. Those without loving families start off with an enormous disadvantage, but I think this is something we have to deal with. I think giving people self-respect is the only solution to crime, drugs, and all these sorts of things.

TOM: But there seems to be a collective confusion about this issue, because our society can't come to an agreement about this.

ELIZABETH: That is true to a certain degree, but part of it is based on the fact that—and I'm going back to the political issues—people who don't have a means to live will turn to doing things that are either unethical or criminal. If they are terribly successful at that, they may gain in self-esteem, unless they are shot dead along the way.

They may find real brotherhood among the people in the groups that do those things.

JOHN: You're never going to stop people from cheating on their income tax because you can't catch them all. They'll stop when people believe that it isn't in accordance with their view of what an honest, good person does. And then they won't do it because the money isn't worth the loss of their self-respect.

ELIZABETH: That goes back to the compassion we were talking about earlier—one of the four kinds of love we were talking about. If you are really a compassionate person, you consider not just your mate and your family, but the far-reaching effects of your behavior on other people. And that's harder and harder because what's depicted in the vivid media is divorced from immediate emotion.

TOM: Is there something you would like to communicate to the younger generations about what's important with respect to love?

ELIZABETH: I think that love is communicated in daily life and one doesn't have to use the word or talk about it. It is communicated by the caring for others that goes on in a close family or among close friends, the demonstration of feeling, and giving aid when things go wrong. There was an example in the newspapers last week about a church being burnt down in the South and the neighbors—not just blacks, but whites as well—giving money and providing emotional support to those who were involved. That's compassion put to work.

It seems to me that adolescents are too focused on

themselves and, for a period of time, many do not include the broader world. But many times in schools and homes an awareness of these things is terribly important. My granddaughter goes to a Quaker school in Pennsylvania, a school which insists upon social service from its adolescents. It has students from twenty-five countries around the world and it turns out not only intellectually well-rounded but also socially and ethically well-rounded graduates because they are taught to care about others in demonstrable ways. I think that is terribly important and can't just be talked about. You can't sit at the breakfast table and explain, "I want you to be a good boy. Now this is how you do it." Young people must have the opportunity to see these values in process—put into action.

TOM: How about you, John?

JOHN: One piece of advice I give my children is to make the distinction between lust and love. I'm not putting down lust. Lust can be a lot of fun, but I don't think it has much to do with love. I think you have to warn teenagers that they are going to experience overwhelming emotions about which they should be a little skeptical because such emotions may not last. If they make a commitment, they should intend that commitment to be lasting. That's why much caution is needed.

TOM: So maybe, in the midst of passion, it's good to interject some serious thoughts?

ELIZABETH: I'm not sure that, during the teenage years, they would see this as necessary. We've had some concern about one of our children with regard to this, but at least the message has been there and sooner or later it will permeate.

TOM: How about people who fall out of love? Is there something that can be done to assist these people?

ELIZABETH: Well, I don't know. I think that John and I differ somewhat on this. We have had many discussions about this because, you see, his wife left him. Although there were many reasons why the marriage wasn't working and hadn't been for some years, he would never have divorced her. I have to believe that divorce is necessary and important in certain circumstances. But I do think the divorce rate is—I was going to say "scandalous"—but that isn't the whole truth. It's scary because it's not clear what it's based on. Perhaps there are just people who get married too rapidly to the wrong people.

JOHN: If someone is beating another, or is cruel in another way, the husband and wife have to realize that they have made a mistake and separate. But it shouldn't be done quickly if there is any basis at all for the marriage. I think they should realize that, if they work through these things together, their marriage will probably be better. I think that, if both parties want to continue a marriage, it will continue. It can be done.

ELIZABETH: But one has to keep in mind here—and I tease John [an Englishman by birth] about this because I've read about this happening in the British upper class—if both parties want to continue, they still may not work at the marriage. They may simply decide to live in the same home and live extremely disparate lives, not have the same friends, not do things together. To me, that has absolutely nothing to do with love and very little to do with marriage. It's just a lousy way to live. Period!

TOM: Is there something you would like to say further about your work and your understanding of love?

ELIZABETH: It's a cliché, but it's absolutely true: Don't marry too young. That's all. But the answer to finding a loving partner is not just age. It's being aware of your needs and why you are marrying and believing that you can satisfy those needs if you wait. I was lonely and wanted to be loved and wanted a family very much. I felt distant from my parents at that time. That's why I married. In three years I had three children, and very shortly after that the marriage fell apart. The question is, as always, How does one satisfy those real needs without doing something that is committing and foolish?

JOHN: I think you should marry your best friend. I think before you get married you really have to find someone with compatible interests and whom you admire and trust. Unfortunately, the sexuality part clouds this, and when one is young this gets muddled by passion, which is terribly unreliable.

ELIZABETH: I think there is one more thing. Kahlil Gibran wrote with great wisdom, "Let there be spaces in your togetherness," and I think that is terribly valuable advice. You are not meant to be clones. You're not going to share everything and you need spaces in your relationship.

TOM: We've talked about the marriage vows of "in sickness and in health." How does one person's unhappiness fit into the notion of love within a marriage?

ELIZABETH: Perhaps it depends upon why you are unhappy.

JOHN: You may have been unhappy before you married or entered into the relationship.

I do think that pain is an unavoidable, essential part of life. I tell my children this and they laugh at me. I say that pain is necessary because it is only when you are at the depths of despair that you develop perspective and learn important things about yourself. I thought of myself as a father and a husband once. When my marriage broke up, I lost this identity, what existentialists call the "empirical ego." At that point, you hit the very bottom of despair. But what happens then is that life still goes on being good, in spite of the pain. The sun shines, the birds sing, the flowers still bloom, and people are still nice. So you're never so frightened again in adversity because you've been in the depths and you've survived. "That which does not overcome me makes me stronger." So Nietzsche wrote and I believe it. I always tell my children, "Never commit suicide," because I felt like it two or three times and I've always been damned glad afterwards that I didn't do it.

ELIZABETH: That's the lesson that one should wish to have early in life—to be terribly unhappy, terribly desperate, and yet not quite go over the edge and quit. Because you learn, when you come back, that the potential for life to be good is always there. That's a very useful early lesson.

JOHN: But more than that. When you think you've lost everything that is important to you, you find that you haven't lost everything, not by any means.

TOM: I'm wondering, for couples, if one partner is suffering and unhappy, whether that can be kind of scary for the other. It makes it difficult to know what to do, whether to stay with the person or run away.

ELIZABETH: There is no question about it. There's a great sense of futility, of helplessness, in a situation like that.

JOHN: I suppose it depends on what you think of the other person. If you think the other is worthy and has contributed, which—if you like—is love, then you say, "This is the time I should be sticking by this person." That I think is the key. If you value the person and he or she gets into a period of difficulty, you decide, "I'm needed." And you're willing to wait and help.

TOM: But without that underlying sense of worth or appreciation, it's going to be very difficult.

JOHN: In those circumstances the essential ingredient—love itself—is missing.

TOM: Thank you so very much for being here with us. I'm very appreciative of the time you spent talking to us about these perplexing, challenging questions about love.

ELIZABETH: You've provoked some thoughts, and we are grateful to you for that.

Postscript

December 30, 1996
Dear Ken and Tom,

Years ago I worked for a woman at a university. We had some rough times in the beginning because she thought I was too independent a worker for her liking, but over the years we had become good friends. At that time she was unhappily married to a man who was quite unable to show her his love or to share much of his life with her. About four years ago she met another man—one who had recently lost his wife (through death)—and the world changed. She left her husband to live and travel with this man, although to keep her conscience clear, she checked in from time to time to see how her husband was doing. (Her husband hardly noticed that she was gone or that she had returned—except that the refrigerator was filled with fresh foods.) This year she sent me a Christmas card that so moved me that I wanted to share it with you who are so interested with the nature of love in old age. Here it is:

The personal peace of the last several years, and the harmony of living with a person who also wants it, have made my second "marriage" a joy I never imagined I would have. The complete sharing, after a previous lifetime of nonsharing (parents, husband, children) is a delight and a revelation. I'm luxuriating in it. I could give more, but I don't need to.

I think about this at night during wakeful periods, of which I have many. But when I attempt to concentrate on something more soporific, I drift back to this fundamental all-encompassing warmth. I don't need anymore.

This would be a very special statement given at any age, I think, but it is especially so since they are in their early eighties!

My love to you both—
ELIZABETH LÉONIE SIMPSON

Postscript

February 6, 1997
Dear Ken and Tom,

I remember pondering, when I was in my late teens, on "the meaning of life." Perhaps ten or so years later I partially answered this question with the conclusion that the meaning of life must be decided by each person individually. And now it has taken me another fifty years of struggling to decide exactly what my own meanings are.

I hope one day soon to write my memoirs so that my children and grandchildren can know something of my life, a life which in so many ways was different from their own—both for better and for worse. I would like to include a summary of the values that were passed to me by my parents and schoolteachers and how they differ from the values that I now hold. In their basic essence they differ very little. Yet my religious persuasion is now much less doctrinaire than that of the boy who attended an Episcopal boarding school in England.

Here, the hopeful writer of memoirs has a problem which must not be uncommon. Now believing that all religious laws and guidance are the work of man, rather than the word of God, there are no hard-and-fast directions available to steer us through our lives. Perhaps this makes life more interesting. Certainly, as the existentialists claim, it produces more anguish. But isn't anguish—or concern— a measure of our value as human beings? An old Chinese proverb says, "It is better to be a crystal broken than a tile intact on the roof top." Are we humans anything of consequence without integrity, bravery, compassion, or—that all-inclusive concept we discussed—love?

When I was younger, I spent much of my time thinking of the future. Now that I am older, I spend much of my time thinking of the past. I have become aware that we get only one chance at life—and very much aware that what seems most valuable is loving, trusting, relationships remembered.

Is it too shallow to hope that we did a fair job and that after we have gone the love we gave will be treasured enduringly by those who were closest to us? That would be Heaven, indeed!

Most cordially,
JOHN WURR

ABRAHAM LEVITSKY

The lamps are different,
but the light is the same.
So many lamps in the dying brain's
lamp shop, —forget about them.
Concentrate on essence, concentrate on Light.
In lucid bliss, calmly smoking off its own holy fire,
the light streams toward you from all things,
all people, all possible permutation of good, evil,
  thought, passion.
The lamps are different,
but the light is the same.
One matter, one energy, one light, one light-mind,
endlessly emanating all things.
One turning and burning diamond,
one, one, one.
Ground yourself, strip yourself down,
to blind loving silence.
Stay there until you see
you are gazing at the light
with its own ageless eyes.

—RUMI

ABRAHAM LEVITSKY

I WAS BORN in 1922. I was raised in the Orthodox Jewish tradition, and my father was a cantor in the synagogue. Judaism never took, but the cultural aspects of being Jewish are deeply ingrained. I have one son and three grandchildren. I feel so fortunate—they're such a delightful family.

I earned a Ph.D. in Clinical Psychology. My career has been in adult psychotherapy, and I currently have a private practice in Berkeley, California. I have studied closely with Frederick (Fritz) Perls and was a past president of the San Francisco Gestalt Institute. My primary interests are integrating hypnosis and psychoanalysis with Gestalt Therapy. My decades of interest in Eastern mysticism have been playing an increasingly important role in my work.

I am a serious student of the Hindu Advaita (nonduality) philosophy; my teacher is Ramesh Balseker of Bombay. I am currently doing fulfilling research for a public talk on the down-to-earth aspects of the transformation or "enlightenment" experience.

TOM: Abe, I'd like to welcome you here to our discussion series "Elders on Love." I realize that it's a very broad topic. We're trying to give the elders an opportunity to speak to those of us of the younger generation about their lives and their reflections on love, spirituality, and community. How can we begin with such an undertaking?

ABE: There's something funny about that question. It appears to me that we can begin by recognizing it as a very, very considerable challenge. I, as the so-called elder, am speaking to younger generations, presuming that I have some sort of knowledge or wisdom to offer and confer. The simple fact is that we have yet to discover whether that's true. That might be a bit of wisdom right there.

TOM: What are your reflections on the influences in your life which have shaped your thinking about love?

ABE: Lord, well, it's an endless question. I think immediately of two aspects of it: one is that which has facilitated my understanding and appreciation of the experience of love, and then the other side of it, that which has interfered with or provided obstacles or roadblocks I've had to overcome in learning about love. With regard to the former, the first thing that comes to mind is my spiritual teacher, Ramesh. One of the things that I love about him is not that he's a Buddha, but he is a teacher and friend. Ramesh is an elderly man who lives in India and who has taught me a great deal. What a pleasure it is to like him, to love him, but also to feel his affection for me, his loyalty to me. When I have turned to him in times of need or stress, the care and the thought that he takes to speak with me through his letters have been models of love and caring.

TOM: How did he enter your life, or how did you enter his?

ABE: Well, when he retired at the age of sixty, he had been director of a very large bank in Bombay. In fact, I think it was a series of banks. In a bookstore he accidentally came across a book which has now become a classic of mysticism by a man named Nisargadatta. He realized that this man, Nisargadatta, lived in his very city, Bombay. He looked at the book, as I and many other people have, and was immediately struck by its tremendous impact on him. So he went to Nisargadatta who lived in a very, very humble abode and who taught groups, classes, and seminars daily. He got acquainted with his teacher and spent several years studying with him, and also became his interpreter. After some two-and-a-half years of that, what we might call the transformation occurred in Ramesh himself. He became enlightened. (The word enlightenment carries a lot of freight. Anytime I use it I tend to talk about it in a way that just pokes around it.) So then Ramesh wrote a book, a commentary on the work of Nisargadatta, which came to my attention in the early eighties.

TOM: What effect has this relationship had on you and have you any reflections about your consciousness at this stage in your life?

ABE: One thing I can report, and with pleasure, is that coincidentally in the last several weeks a couple of people who are close to me have remarked that I feel lighter to them. This comment is music to my ears because there are two sides to my character: the light side that tends to clown and make jokes, and then the rather heavy, serious somber side that frankly gets on my nerves a little bit. So to be told that I feel lighter, and also to feel that in myself, feels like a triumph.

TOM: What has changed? What are people noticing?

ABE: Well, a) it's not easy to say, and b) it's a long story. I think I've come to terms with some elements of myself a little bit more successfully, which just makes me feel better, more buoyant, more confident. I think I can say validly that my "spiritual studies" have played an important role in this.

Let me give a bit of recent history and background. Right now it's August 1996. Early this year, in the middle of January, I went to Bombay to spend two weeks with my teacher, Ramesh, and I attended his seminars daily. I was in very good spirits at the time and I participated actively in the seminars. Ramesh was very glad to see me, as he always is, and I was glad to see him. However, in spite of my decades-long interest in these studies, I didn't realize at the time the extent to which I was being self-deceptive. In the discussion groups I was talking a very good game. But it was only afterwards, after I returned to the States and was reflecting on what had happened there, that I realized that there was a good deal of self-deception, a certain amount of posturing—as they say, a lot of show and not much go. After all, I had read enough and listened to him enough that I knew the verbal formulations very well. To the group members, I guess, it sounded like I knew what I was talking about. I thought I knew what I was talking about. But what was missing was a deeper appreciation and also the experience of what I was talking about. I realized I had kidded myself.

TOM: What was the nature of your discussions?

ABE: The discussions were essentially about the meaning of enlightenment and self-transcendence.

TOM: Would you say that your teacher, Ramesh, has influenced you with respect to your thoughts about love?

ABE: Yes, enormously. I'm remembering some writings on Nisargadatta in which he takes a very radical position, a position which I've come to appreciate more and more as time goes on. His point is that unless one achieves "ego-transcendence" or "self-transcendence," one is very limited in the capacity for love. Until one achieves that, one is involved, largely unconsciously, with defending the self, enhancing the self, protecting the self, polishing the self-image, et cetera. All of these are the opposite of love and interfere with truly being with others.

TOM: Is there something that we can teach people about self-deception that will help in developing more genuine love?

ABE: We speak about "the prescription of non-prescription." This means to have a profound interest in the question and to recognize that there is hardly anything in life that is more important.

TOM: Instead of fostering a deeper appreciation of that important value, it seems that we go about other business and fall asleep in some sense.

ABE: Almost everything in our society, in our culture, conspires to keep us asleep in this respect.

TOM: Humanity appears to be engaged in types of consciousness that leave us confused, angry, bitter, and hateful. How can we cultivate more consciousness of love on a daily basis?

ABE: There is a tragic absence of love, caring, concern for one's fellow human being in the world today to such an extent that, in my opinion, most of the world is rather insane and self-destructive. I seriously believe that we live in apocalyptic times and that the forces of destruction and evil and nonlove and absurdity have reached a level of intensity which is unspeakable, almost beyond the pale.

TOM: What can we do to jar ourselves into awareness?

ABE: Suppose you translate the question "What can we do?" into "What can I do?" or "What do I do?" I then imagine that most thinking, sensitive people have the very uncomfortable feeling that "I don't do enough."

What do you think follows if you believe, with your heart and soul, that we live in apocalyptic times?

TOM: I think many of us feel a greater sense of urgency about doing something, whatever that might be. I'd like to ask whether there is some discipline, some concentration that we can apply on a daily basis to keep us on task, focused, and more connected to what's truthful or what's important.

ABE: Such things as attitude, reflection, contemplation, perhaps meditation I believe are very important. But even more important are action, community consciousness, and community commitment. It occurs to me to take a lead from the feminist movement and the work feminists did in setting up consciousness-raising groups. In doing that, I believe they made a very important, radical, and everlasting contribution to public affairs in this country. Consciousness-raising applied more broadly might well take the form of what I'd call community-consciousness-raising groups or citizenship-consciousness-raising groups. In these groups people working in the same office or working in the same factory or living on the same street might get together in groups of eight or fifteen or so people. They'd ask themselves questions similar to those asked by women in the early years of the feminist movement, questions such as: "What does it mean to be a person? How do I establish a good self-image as a person? How do I re-empower myself as a person? What are those forces in society which get in the way of my self-respect as a person?" Analogously, people involved in community-consciousness-raising would ask such questions as: "What is it like truly to feel myself a member of this community? What do I have to say about what happens in this community, both the local community and the wider community?" To think about and discuss issues along these lines and to re-empower ourselves is called spiritual politics. And that's the closest I come to a prescription of advice.

TOM: Your comments raise the issue of how we can help people feel connected to a sense of community.

ABE: These groups would begin by talking and exchanging ideas, but it's a serious error to be limited to talk; one must undertake some kind of collective action. I am inspired by the thinking of the theologian Paul Tillich, who talked about two kinds of courage. One is courage to be as a part of. Interestingly enough, it takes courage to be a part of a group. The other kind of courage is the courage to be as oneself. So these two basic vectors need to be simultaneously recognized and attended to in order to achieve a sense of wholeness—individuation and individuality on the one hand, and broad collective group identification on the other hand.

TOM: So there's a dynamic between the individual, the community, and then back?

ABE: But don't underemphasize the back. The individual in the community and then the individual within himself or herself. Because it's one helluva trick to be yourself and a part of at the same time. Isn't one of the mysteries of marriage to be in a close relationship with another person—a relationship which is affectionate, dynamic, growing—and at the same time still be one's own person?

I believe that if you can get people seriously interested in thinking about exchanging ideas along these lines that you've made a marvelous contribution.

TOM: Do you think, though, in order to get the individual excited about committing to the community needs, that somehow the community has to end up loving the individual, valuing the individual or individual's participation?

ABE: I believe that the answer to that lies in self-regard and self-love, because when those are achieved, then it follows as a natural consequence that there is love and respect for others.

TOM: So if you have self-love, then you yourself have some kind of intrinsic appreciation for what you do. You don't necessarily have to have the community lauding you or loving you for what you do. You just do it out of sheer joy.

ABE: Yes, we are social creatures, and we simultaneously require our own regard and the regard of others. But all of this is in the context of relative or conventional thinking. However, spiritual discussion transcends some of the stuff we've just touched on, and then goes into a domain which is rather different.

TOM: Would you care to say more about that?

ABE: I talk about it with hesitancy because, to many people, it sounds incomprehensible or unreal or terribly idealistic or just plain misguided.

TOM: But maybe people need to hear that there is a transcendent level of activity or of discussion. You're talking about something that may be very foreign for them to grasp.

ABE: Rather foreign. In recent years, with the growth of interest in meditation and in Eastern ideologies, there is more concern and interest with what I'm calling self-transcendence. Let me try to summarize it in a little phrase. When we say in Spanish "Vaya con Dios," or "Go with God," one translation of that is "May you be granted the knowledge that you are not an individual." Doesn't that sound a little odd?

TOM: How is it odd for you?

ABE: Because the notion that I, that we, that you are individuals is so deeply ingrained in the marrow of our bones, as it were. It's very much like the way people felt pre-1492. The world was flat then, was it not? You just looked around you and you saw it with your own eyes: The world is flat. If you offered somebody on the west coast of Spain a ship in which to sail west for X hundred miles, they're not interested in doing that because, the world being flat, they're going to fall off the edge. That the world is flat seems to be a fact that's observable through one's senses. Now in a very similar way, psychologically, we grow up in a society in which both social belief and all of our senses tell us that we're individuals. And along comes some idea that questions something so innately ingrained.

TOM: Is there a practice that goes along with realizing that we're not individuals as such?

ABE: There are different schools of thought. Some people say you can practice and some people say you can't. There are those who say, "Stand on your head," or "Learn how to breathe," or "Meditate eight years in a cave," or "Be obedient to the master." Then there are people like my teacher who say, "Doubt it very much."

TOM: Do you find that when you are filled with the feeling of love that you experience an ideal state that serves as some kind of an overriding function for you?

ABE: Remember that I've been talking about two domains. There is the ordinary "conventional" domain and, when I feel loving in that domain, there is no question that it's self-rewarding. Love's a beautiful feeling, a nice feeling. It's a helluva lot nicer than to feel bitter, sorrowful, antagonistic, distant, remote, unconcerned, critical, and so on. So it's much more beautiful and much more satisfying to be in a loving space than in some other space. But there I refer to the ordinary, the conventional domain. However, in this other, "higher" domain where I can say, "May you be blessed with the knowledge that you are not an individual," here it gets both mysterious and poetic. Here, you are not loving, you are love. There are some who can say that from experience and there are others, like myself, who only know about it and take it somewhat on faith.

TOM: Are you also saying something about the quality of the mind of a person in that "higher" domain, that to be love would suggest that you have an intuitive grasp of how to conduct yourself? Would there then be a true alignment?

ABE: It goes further than that. If you are that quality, there is nothing to align. If you are that quality, then you continue to be that quality as you breathe in and out. That's the point of it, that's the beauty of it, that's the mystery of it.

TOM: One thing we were attempting to do with this series of interviews is to have people like you speak to us of the younger generation, to make some observations or suggestions about pitfalls and situations that might interfere with the potential for becoming a truly loving person.

ABE: The pitfalls are innumerable and all around us. I guess the major ones are what I'd call the major seductions: notions of wealth, power, fame, recognition, success. These are all goals towards which most of us strive with the belief that, if we achieve them, we will have achieved something very important, we'll be happier and more content, et cetera. There may be some truth to that. But in my opinion, they are essentially seductions and distractions. From what are they distractions? Distractions from the mystical and illusive thing that I've been talking about: self-transcendence. This realm of the mysterious, the mystic, and mystical is only partially understood by our reasoning, logical minds.

TOM: Is there something about the mysterious that our society needs to talk about? Is an appreciation for the mysterious or the numinous an ingredient that is missing?

ABE: The answer has to be "yes." The trick seems to be how to say "yes" in some way that is not cheap, that does not trivialize it. The mysterious is a mystery, and our ordinary minds are limited in dealing with such domains. Something else called "intuitive perception" seems to be required. I think that the twentieth century, with its emphasis on invention, technology, science, and reasoning has led us away from the importance of the intuitive.

TOM: I realize that there are some people who really don't want to change and are content with being in their particular state of consciousness or state of pain or what have you. So then why should we talk about trying to change or raise people's consciousness?

ABE: Well, that reminds me of a story. In World War I there was a young socialist whose name was Jimmy Higgins. He'd get up on his soap box every night and say, "Socialism is inevitable." So finally a person in the audience got impatient and said, "If it's so goddamn inevitable, why don't you just shut up and let it just be inevitable?"

Jimmy Higgins replied, "It's because I come here every night and tell you that it's inevitable that it's inevitable." So the same role has been played by every religious leader. Christ, Buddha, religious leaders of all times have been in one way or another saying to people, "Hey folks, guess what? You think you're awake, but you're really asleep."

TOM: Maybe that is enough—giving people a sense of uncertainty about their state of awakeness.

ABE: If you can plant that idea seriously into people's consciousness, that what they think is being awake is in a very serious sense asleep, then you have taken a giant step. If you say, "You are really asleep," they say, "Wow, I thought I was awake and this guy's telling me I'm asleep." Eventually, they may come to ask, "Well, if I take it seriously, what might it feel like to be awake and what are the limitations of being asleep?" Now when you start talking like that, then you have come to the state described in the words of another great guru of our times, Ramana Maharshi: "When the mind turns in upon itself in that way, then the head is in the tiger's mouth and the tiger will never let go."

TOM: What do you think of the activities of transcendental meditation groups who meditate for world peace or to alleviate the crime of large metropolitan areas?

ABE: I suspect they're barking up the wrong tree. I suspect that they are trying to substitute, in a sense, mental magic for practical action. At the same time, their concern with these issues, I believe, is a very important contribution. They make the assumption that, if we all meditate at

the same time, we can make some change. I am not prepared to say a great deal about that.

TOM: Let me go back to the people in your life that have
influenced you. I'm curious what it is about Ramesh that has
influenced you or touched you?

ABE: You have to remember I met Ramesh kind of late
in my life. I have known him only for the last ten years.
He is a teacher whom I would not have sought out if I had
not previously had other teachers.

Many, many influences in my life in one way or another moved me in this direction. I think my Jewishness,
with its concern for morality, is very important here. At
the same time, my Jewishness was a terribly mixed blessing. It took a lot of time and energy and struggle and
whatnot to come to terms with that. Then, having grown
up in the Depression years in New York City, which was a
center of leftist Marxist thinking, inclined me in the direction of social reform and social morality. Once again,
that was a mixed blessing. I had to unlearn an awful lot
of the foolishness, the one-sidedness, the blindness, the
just plain idiocy that was associated with some of that kind
of thinking. Then, in college when I got interested in psychology and psychotherapy, my professor Abraham
Maslow was a very important influence. So all of these influences somehow come together.

TOM: So is Ramesh such a teacher?
ABE: He's graduate work.

TOM: Is there something about his character that you admire, that has shaped your own character?

ABE: An important thing for me about Ramesh as a teacher is that he was a worldly person. Many spiritual teachers seem to have been living on a mountaintop or in a cave. Ramesh was a bank director. So he is very, very much a man of the world; he's practical and knows his way around. At the same time that he was a bank director with authority and responsibility, he was a very soft, sweet considerate person. That's quite a rarity. He combines in himself those qualities of character with his high intelligence. From the time that he was a youngster he kind of knew that he had in himself this drive to be a spiritual seeker. Although he studied with a number of teachers and, under them, practiced periods of meditation, he also knew that that was not the real thing. It was only when he met his teacher that he knew that "Ah, here was the great opportunity."

TOM: How important is it to have a teacher? Some people feel that it's critical that one have a guru, a spiritual master, whereas others say just the opposite.

ABE: If you have a fine teacher, you're lucky. I personally don't think I could have achieved much without a very fine teacher.

TOM: Why is that?

ABE: Some people have more effective and powerful inner teachers and some people need to be taught. Without external help, I don't think I could have gone very far. I have a ways to go, a very considerable ways to go.

TOM: I'm intrigued by that observation. Where do you see yourself going? What is the implied distance here?

ABE: I'll remind you of my translation of "Go with God." I said one translation of "Go with God" is "May you be granted the knowledge that you are not an individual." I have not yet been granted that. But the beauty of the existence of a person such as my teacher Ramesh is that he experiences that he is not an individual.

TOM: But I gather you've seen some progress?

ABE: I feel that. Yes. I feel it.

TOM: Is there anything you could share with us as to how your work with clients relates to teaching about love?

ABE: Much of my work centers on it in the use of such concepts as self-regard, self-compassion, improved self-image, awareness of self-hate, becoming aware that self-hate contains within itself tremendous power. If there is that power, that power is in the individual who is powerless and yet who has within some kind of negative power which is turned against his- or herself. So to make a person aware of that and to work with him or her in such a way that that powerful energy can then be used to go out constructively rather than to belittle and chop oneself down is a central focus of my work.

TOM: What you would like to share with the younger generations, some advice, some teaching perhaps? When you think about your life and what you'd like to pass on as your legacy, what might that be?

ABE: The thing that comes to mind is never forget that we are one human family.

TOM: That's very nice. Abe, I want to thank you for coming here today and sharing your thoughts and views on love.

Truly, I am very honored by your willingness to participate in this discussion.

ABE: Thank you. For me, it has proved to be surprisingly fun, interesting, challenging, and stimulating.

Postscript

March 4, 1997
Dear Ken and Tom,

What a welcome surprise! I have been more affected than I anticipated by my participation in the "Elders on Love" project. I approached the matter with skepticism, and it is still my frank opinion that the discussion we had as a group was no great contribution to the literature or history of thought. But sometimes a seemingly simple event or thought can make worthwhile many hours of effort. And hearing from Pauline that in her early nineties she is vital, enthusiastic, and full of juices was an explosion—delightful, stirring, inspiring!

It happens that these discussions come at a fortunate time for me. A combination of circumstances makes me more open to considerations of the nature of love than I have ever been. So I, at age seventy-five, can say with Pauline that I feel fortunate having in my life what feels like a sufficiency of love: from marriage, family, friends, colleagues, work.

It was not always thus. Quite the contrary. I can say with some objectivity that my present situation has come about via fearsome struggle. I have easily endured my share of life's hammerblows. That my journey has taken this turn, I would not have predicted.

As to my present outlook, I am reminded of a remark by Frederick Perls. He was full of quips and one that has remained in my memory is, "I no longer distinguish between age and youth." I wouldn't go that far. Yet, at the same time, it is hugely gratifying to note how much of his attitude has gotten into my very bones.

Accordingly, I have many reservations as to whether "we elders" have so much to teach the younger generations about love. In initiating and organizing this project, you, our two "young" coordinators, have displayed qualities of mature thinking and impressive dedication which would be a credit to anyone. You demonstrate a great depth of connection to the life-force. May it be contagious.

It has been evident for some time that growing up in an apocalyptic age has made many of our youth frightened and alienated, while others have been imbued with the urgent necessity of learning broad human values as a condition of survival itself. This thought has been repeated many times. But we cannot be concerned about repetitiousness when our very survival hangs in the balance. Can we urge and educate each other sufficiently to have courage, sagacity, and a willingness to take risks that are undoubtedly necessary if the terrifying tides of destruction are to be stemmed?

The question is still open.

ABRAHAM LEVITSKY

March 7, 1997
Dear Ken and Tom,

A few days after I wrote that last line, "The question is still open," I got to thinking. Here's how my thinking went:

Here I am batting my gums about the "terrifying tides," talking about nothing less than THE END, Finis, Finito. And, numbed into the same sensibility as the rest of us, I come up with a mighty cool line, "The question is still open." Nice, very nice. And nauseating.

This lovey-love stuff is just fine. But it's not enough. What would I feel if my family and I were being brutalized by Nazis before each other's eyes?

But hey, hold it! There's no "if" about that. It's not a conjecture. It not only has happened, it's happening daily. It's happening now. What will stop the bestiality from going on—and on?

Doesn't the burning love of life and fellowmen need to give birth to an equally holy anger—anger at the beasts? Don't we need to keep constantly before our eyes the "Howl" of Allen Ginsberg: "I saw the best minds of my generation destroyed by madness, starving, hysterical naked . . ." Don't we need to burn into our brains the unspeakable images of the "Last Judgment" in order to oppose the fury of mindless hate with our greater determination for life's continuance?

So far our soft lives have prepared us for little more than reading the noble sentiments of others. I don't know yet whether I am capable yet of the kind of hymn to compassion as sounded by the extraordinary Vietnamese Buddhist fighter for peace, Thich Nhat Hanh. In one of his poems he says, "Hatred will never let you face the beast in man . . ." Considering what he has endured, this is staggering. Perhaps if you or I had waded through rivers of our loved ones' blood, then we might find such superhuman strength. Let's see what we're capable of when we hurt enough!

ABRAHAM LEVITSKY

PAULINE E. THOMPSON

Though I speak with the tongues of men and of angels,
and have not charity,
I am become as sounding brass, or a tinkling cymbal.
And though I have the gift of prophecy,
and understand all mysteries, and all knowledge,
and though I have all faith so that I could
  remove mountains
but have not charity, I am nothing.
And though I bestow all my goods to feed the poor,
and though I give my body to be burned,
and have not charity,
it profiteth me nothing.

—PAUL, 1 CORINTHIANS 13

Love of God is pure
when joy and suffering inspire
an equal degree of gratitude.

—SIMONE WEIL

PAULINE E. THOMPSON

I WAS BORN in 1905, in Spokane, Washington. I graduated from North Central High School in Spokane in 1921, with honors; I had taken the Classical Course, with the intention, originating at about age seven, to become a missionary doctor. I obtained a bachelor's degree from Washington State College in 1927 and a master's in 1930. I also have a second master's from Teachers College, Columbia University, New York City. (My employer wanted someone with an Eastern degree!) I matriculated for my doctorate in 1931 and received it in 1947.

Meanwhile, I secured my nursing license from Bellevue Hospital School of Nursing. I enlisted in World War II in the U.S. Army Nurse Corps and served mainly in Paris during the Battle of the Bulge. My non-army nursing was largely in psychiatry.

I taught at all grade levels from kindergarten through grade 13, including the mentally retarded, the gifted, and in a school for the blind, for thirty-five years. I was the first school psychologist in Berkeley in 1948.

I had a year of Freudian analysis in 1941–42, and entered Jungian analysis in 1949. I remained in analysis until 1966, thereafter maintaining my relationship with my analyst until her death in 1980. I have practiced as a psychotherapist, and have become a life member of the American Psychological Association.

In a world full of malcontents (I was one myself for years) many are saying bitterly, "Why me? Why must I suffer so? Why does God allow it? There is no God." In such a world, I still say "Why me?" but now I mean, "Why am I so blessed? Why do I find my life so beautiful, so expanding, so secure and unafraid, so everlasting?" I have written such words because I feel an obligation to society— to my fellow men (and all men are my brothers)—to share the ever-increasing joy and fulfillment of my old age.

TOM: Pauline, I'd like to welcome you to our series "Elders on Love." Maybe we could begin by talking about the atmosphere in which you were raised and how this influenced you.

PAULINE: I grew up supposing that everyone who grew up in a church-going environment was experiencing the same religious life as I. But since then I have discovered that my feelings and motives and perceptions were much less secular than other people's. I lacked the usual Christian attitude, which is not felt so spiritually. Unconsciously, I felt that my love of God transcended my love of people and things. I felt love of God transcends, literally, human experience and is not to be confused with it. In my mind, incarnation is the love of what we call God. It transforms us human animals so that we finally become totally aware that we are the only divine animal. We're the only animal that loves the unseen as well as the seen, that can image the abstract. These are distinct and remarkable properties, human properties: to see the invisible and remember what we have seen.

I am a child of the entire twentieth century, being born in 1905, conceived in 1904 (following Mother's miscarriage of a female fetus sometime between 1900 and 1904). In this outer world we are seeing what it is like to have a life that is not spiritual. Incarnation has not taken place with most people. As I often have put it, most people don't itch and, therefore, most people justly refuse to scratch.

I grew up in a rare religious atmosphere, not knowing it was rare. One Christmas I made Santa Claus a necktie which became the occasion of Mother's explaining his psyche to me in such a way that, later, I felt the same spiritual affinity to God and His son that I had to Santa Claus. Love was a primary value to me long before I knew that it is the primary value.

My mother lived a deeply religious life. I don't mean merely creed, though I thought so at the time. Truly religious, truly re-tied, re-aligned, *re-ligio* to God. Consequently, I have had many incredible inner experiences and relationships! I wrote some haiku on this subject a few years ago. My favorite one read: "Do you believe in miracles? / Yes of course, I am one." My earlier secular life became more complex as life situations became increasingly more complex. I have lived the good life only in moments as life itself has been corrupted into problems which have become totally exaggerated out of all reason and sense. I cannot help feeling that we are at the end of an age, and that a long, long time will pass before the new age comes to bloom. But I'm an incurable optimist because I'm still convinced that life will come into bloom again. Even if we don't accomplish anything (as my religious outlook sees and seeks it) in this temporal existence, nothing is lost. As some physicists say, "Nothing is lost; it's just transformed," so I feel equally about the inner or psychic life. I was thinking about the life attitude of a chrysalis. When a chrysalis knows it's time to become a butterfly, if it acted the way we humans do, it would try to hang onto being a chrysalis until the last ditch. We know that eggs and larvae and worms and tadpoles die into larger life; we don't know that we do, too.

TOM: Maybe most people don't have a sense of themselves as butterflies that have evolved from something or are evolving towards something. They don't have a clear vision of who they are.

PAULINE: That's the central problem. We talk about love and we measure it in terms of what we do for other people. But the basis of love is that we love this miracle that we are. We ourselves. It's the difference between Self and selfish, "-ish." "Ish" is a suffix; it's not the real thing: Our selves are just like us; they are not us. I can only try to be like my God-image, but I don't fancy that I am God.

We can't have love and pride at the same time. I try not to be proud; I cannot be both proud and loving, and I'd rather love.

TOM: Could we say that somehow people become more enamored with the feeling of pride than with the feeling of love?

PAULINE: Yes. I don't have anything really except my own soul. If I don't know I have a soul, then I haven't got anything at all. Still, I haven't said it right yet. I should have said, "If I am not a soul, I'm nothing."

TOM: There seems to be such a basic confusion that exists for people between loving and the prideful imaging of love. Can we ask ourselves whether or not we are in a loving state? Do you think we can develop a consciousness of love in the day-to-day?

PAULINE: I'm very interested in what you're doing with these interviews because you're discussing human relationships as if they had a value and a meaning and a utility in the way we live our lives. You are incarnating love into our behavior, not just our ideas. You're exemplifying the highest product, as I see it, of the temperament that says, "Yes, I understand about love, I see how essential it is to happiness, I find it a fulfilling way of life, but I don't know how to express it." You are the first people I've found whom I am sure are consciously looking. I have looked, unconsciously most of my life, but I have looked. Now I have found you.

I can prove that I was born looking. I still remember the first light that was in my bedroom when I was a child. My father had designed the house and had built my bedroom with my window high up on the wall so I couldn't fall out of it. We moved into that house when I was three or four months old. Before age five or thereabouts, I remember Dad often carrying me upstairs, and I would say my prayers on my knees with my mother beside me, and then I would be tucked in and kissed goodnight by both parents.

But when I got to be old enough, I kissed my parents downstairs and then went upstairs alone and in the dark. My last sight was of Venus shining outside the window. I suppose it was Venus—it could have been Aldebaran then, when the star was visible. I know I have felt the influence of the stars ever since, though I think I had forgotten that particular view of them until I had my "big dream" of "Bertha" in 1954.

TOM: Looking through that window at Venus must have touched you or instilled some feeling in you that was important.

PAULINE: Different sorts of feelings. I was only an "animal" then; I didn't yet have an established ego.

When at age fifty-four I had my dream of Bertha (and the star of Bethlehem), it brought back the memory of the time when I was about twelve. (More decades would pass before I remembered Venus at my window when I was four or five.) I looked down my uncle's well when we went there on a visit on a hot summer day—it was really hot, over a hundred. In broad daylight I looked down into his well and there was a star at the bottom of it. So I went inside and asked Mother about it, and she explained to me that the starlight was always there. The only reason I couldn't see it was that there was too much daylight intervening. Only when you get rid of the nearby temporal light can you see the starlight.

So years later I had the dream. In the dream, I'm on my journey, and I am on my knees in front of a roadside cross, and the Star of Bethlehem and the Star of Aldebaran both shine overhead. (Aldebaran is one of the stars in our galaxy of the first magnitude. You can see the star Aldebaran with the naked eye—it's the red eye of Taurus, the bull.) In my dream, the bigger and higher star was the star of Bethlehem, the light of God, and the other was my human star—Aldebaran was a man in the children's story where I met him.

TOM: What feelings were you left with after this dream?

PAULINE: This dream simply marked the fact that consciousness is necessary. If you don't know something, you can't act on it. But what's really necessary is to do something about it after you become conscious. And I have been privileged to live long enough to discover a little of how to do it.

I had intended to write an autobiography, and I have the makings of it. But I haven't written it and I probably won't live long enough to do it. I'm too busy living it to write it down. I've got too much living to do. Why should I break off living to find some time to crystallize my past visions?

I'm realizing more aspects of the future in the last four years than I did in the other almost ninety. At one time I read a definition of old age as being "the sad process of going down a corridor watching the doors close as you go forward." But my experience has been that my old age has been an opportunity to see myself going toward the light with doors *opening* on both sides of the corridor as I go forward. My past accumulates up to now, and the farther back and outward it becomes conscious, the farther ahead I can extrapolate.

TOM: You seem to be saying that you're learning to hold onto, to become aware of your memories.

PAULINE: The best way of loving is to become conscious of that for which you have loved yourself. There is a subtle difference between my consciousness and my conscientiousness. I really feel that the voice of conscience is incarnating. I am learning to know, and then to know that I know, and then learning to know what to do about it. And that means that the voice of conscience is the voice of God. I have learned to feel that the voice of conscience is simply a matter of learning more about how to love and then living it.

A lot of people feel they have the problem of having "wandered." I have one new friend at present who does not like God and has the courage to say so. I keep trying to tell her that she doesn't like the God-image she has. It just doesn't make sense that she loves Jesus (as she claims) and does not love God. Jesus is God's creation whom He created expressly to show us what love is. It's impossible to hold this image of Jesus and, at the same time, hold the God-image of an old guy with a long beard and a fierce temper. At least my friend has Jesus in her mind, if not in her hungry heart. This generation mostly has nothing; and they are continually asking, "Does God really exist?"

TOM: So what would you make of your friend? What would you say is blocking her?

PAULINE: She's trying to get out of the way the namby-pamby, good-for-nothing God who does nothing but lose His temper and exact vengeance. I don't know how many times I've read Jung's "Answer to Job." But I say that if I can't love the evil that God created by creating good, if "there is no evil," if God could take all the evil out of mankind if He wanted to (so that we instantly become good as God(?!) with no labor whatsoever on our part), if any individual is all good or conversely some individuals are all bad, none of these statements are true. What God did say to Job is the simple truth that we are all too small and He is too great for us to comprehend. If we don't have a God-image that says that the supernatural is supernatural—if, indeed, we don't believe in the super-natural—then I figure we're nothing as people. We are only nice animals.

TOM: There are many people who can't grasp the super-natural.

PAULINE: If I can't grasp it, if it doesn't interest me, if my attitude is "I've got enough on my plate already—don't bother me," then I am a sheep. And it's all right to be a sheep: I need only one shepherd if I live in a flock. If I don't itch, it's okay for me not to scratch.

TOM: But can we teach love?

PAULINE: No. No. No. No. We can't teach any personal value.

TOM: We can't teach sheep how to love?

PAULINE: That's right, and the reason we can't do it is that we don't admit that we don't know ourselves. How can you give anything to anybody else if you don't have it yourself? All this talk about self-esteem! Are you going to do good for somebody else at your own expense? I'm not doing this to be good; it is good that saving my own soul is the best way I can serve the common good.

TOM: So you're saying we can't teach love, but we know that people can find love, they can make good things hap-pen to themselves, they can see that it matters how they deal with life events or situations. Are there rituals that we can teach?

PAULINE: We can't teach it. We can do it . . .

TOM: What can we do to help people make the feeling of love more permanent, more present, more continuous?

PAULINE: I don't think we can do one single solitary thing except to do it ourselves.

TOM: So there are no tricks to it?

PAULINE: You have to do it yourself.

TOM: And by our actions we can inspire people.

PAULINE: Look at our last election. We're having another election in a couple of months and we'll be just as evil then as we are now. San Francisco voted three bond issues so that they can extend payments to another generation. We not only overlook the kids now so much that we're having prisons built for them instead of schools, we've done the same thing to our grandchildren, and now we're doing the same thing to our great-grandchildren. We have sold the souls of our kids' future long before they are even born. Our kids won't have souls to sell. Or to find. Or to live by. Physical bodies with no souls, ever. We've killed them in utero.

TOM: Given what you've been saying, what would you like to communicate to the younger generations about love?

PAULINE: I figure that my life is what I contribute. My life, I'm here. I'm evidence that it happens. It's not something to read in a book, it's not theory. I believe in love as the most potent and in a real sense the only potent reality. Love requires consciousness of self which, in turn, requires logos, truth, and knowledge. Loving is the fruit of my labor. My life is a laboratory and love is my tool. If I don't love, I don't belong, I'm not really alive.

TOM: You're saying that you are putting your life forward as an example.

PAULINE: That's why I'm so thrilled by your project. You don't say you care, you do care.

TOM: I'd like to talk about freedom. Does a lack of freedom interfere with the ability to love?

PAULINE: The guy that spends his life in solitary prison can't feel very hopeful that his life has any social meaning. The only thing that makes it possible for him to be more free than the jailer that put him there is the freedom that lies between his ears. I'll never forget the shock I went through when I was visiting Calcutta and a tour took us out to a prison known as the "Black Hole of Calcutta." The tour guide let us go in one by one if we so wished. (Only three of us chose to go in.) They closed the door on each of us for one minute. I recall the feeling that you're there in the unbearable darkness and you'll never get out, and that you've been reduced to something worse than death. But some prisoners stayed there for months and even years. We're talking about possession of their own souls. No matter how degrading the circumstances, human beings have survived, so we know mankind is capable of love beyond any measure we have for it.

TOM: It seems, with our complicated lives, modern pressures, and the deprivation and suffering that exist globally or collectively, that love is shutting down.

PAULINE: Well, the expressions of love are shutting down because they have had so little outlet. There's so little consciousness of love left compared to what we were born into. I remember my childhood jump ropes and the big swing that all the neighbors in the block put up out in our backyard, and the sense of all the parents parenting us all.

TOM: I can feel the purity of those moments, but it seems like that is very hard for us to capture today.

PAULINE: You're bringing in the time factor. We measure things in terms of our own lives, and our own lives aren't even a tenth as alive as we could make them. If my present consisted only of now—but, thank God, it doesn't! My present goes back to a real honest-to-God feeling of loving families, ages old. Real once. Real living skeletons of Lucy and her mate and her child, thirty thousand years ago. And that's paleontology, physical remains, bones. Physicists say billions of years preceded human life.

TOM: It sounds as if we need to be aware that we stand upon a connection to a past that is very old. Maybe it would be helpful for all of us to be able to recapture those feelings of love and the ties to the past and our ancestors.

PAULINE: That's why I feel it's so important for me to speak and why it's so important for people like you to listen. Because I have found that up until the past three or four years, I could talk my head off and it didn't do any good; nobody wanted to listen. That's because I couldn't find the right audience for what I had to say, couldn't find an audience that wanted to know what I wanted them to hear.

TOM: Maybe we need to teach people how to be a better audience, how to listen. But that is difficult because you have to teach people how to be present, truly present.

PAULINE: Actually, we teach people how not to be

present. Most good teachers, unfortunately, are not themselves good listeners. We need to teach people to develop
a sense that what they say is worth saying. I don't think
my way of life is better than anybody else's way of life. I
just know it's better for me, so I must keep on saying it
even if my audiences are afraid to hear me.

TOM: Let's talk for a moment about love and community.
Have you seen communities that are loving?

PAULINE: Well, I feel that the creeds by which people
live are not loving. I don't try to tell a Mormon how to be
a Seventh Day Adventist or a Christian how to be a
Buddhist. I try to talk (as well as live) universal love.

But I'm saying look at a *whole* scenario. I read recently
about New England colonists, Puritans, who came over
and colonized an area where they had no problem with
the Indians because the Indians had almost totally died off
in a serious smallpox epidemic. Previous colonizers had
given the Indians blankets which had been used by victims of smallpox. The current colonizers wrote that they
figured this epidemic was the gift of God to them. He had
removed the menace of the Indians, because they had all
died of smallpox. Knowing is no good if you don't take
the right steps about it. To infect the Indians with smallpox was not loving.

TOM: Have you seen cultures or societies or communities
that seem to do a better job?

PAULINE: I see a lot of them, and I see us daily, hourly,
by the minute, trying to destroy them, and succeeding. I
do think that we have passed the point of no return. The

only reason that I find loving enough for me individually is that I don't have to go along with the group. If I have found one other person who is really looking, if his eye-hole is the same as mine, if we get the same angle on what we're looking at, then it doesn't matter how many trillion other people there are who don't see it. We have the living evidence that we are not alone. And even if you are alone, you're still you. I'm not saying that I'm the only person who is right. But I must try to be the person whom it is right for me to be.

TOM: Are you saying, though, that there is a tendency for the destruction of cultures of love, societies of loving people?

PAULINE: The trend is to do away with love: "Don't be sentimental. It's too difficult. Face reality. Stand on your own feet. Don't put up with anybody else. If you can make a profit, make it." Then if you don't die of starvation, that's because you've managed properly. We don't have the loving attitude that Franklin had toward his fellow "civil disobedients," when he said, "Let us all hang together lest we all hang separately."

TOM: I hear you saying that we should be very aware of the dangers and evils that crush love.

PAULINE: I said earlier there was nothing you could do to teach love. I'm wrong. There's nothing to do in the way of teaching love unless you're a lover. That's what you're supposed to do if you want love. I'm the only person in my circle of friends who is not an artist. So I wondered why I thought I belonged there, and why I wanted to be with these friends, and why they tolerated me. I finally realized that my life itself is my art. You're thanking me for being interviewed. I'm thanking you with possibly even greater purpose, for listening to me. You make it real. All you have to do is listen. But your listening is a talent that costs you a lot, and you're willing to pay the price because you find it worth it.

TOM: I'd like to say that this process has been most remarkable for me. You've responded in your own way to my questions, and I have been pleasantly surprised by what you've come forward with.

PAULINE: You can see this urge in every normally minded child, the wish to know. Mother said my brother when he was growing up drove her absolutely crazy. He was seven years older than I. One day they walked across the Post Street Bridge in Spokane. Mother decided she would keep count beginning when they set foot on the bridge of how many times he asked "Why?" before they got to the other end. More than forty times, I've forgotten the exact number. That's the child. The Bible says, "What father will give them a stone when they ask for bread?" And the answer is that most people will give children stones instead of bread. They do this because they have nothing but stones to give. And I take that as part of my sin.

TOM: How so?

PAULINE: Because I'm a part of the collective grief that still doesn't know how to force the production of bread. You can't do it by force. You've got to do it by love! But how are you going to get love if you haven't got it?

TOM: Is there something we can do about the collective grief?

PAULINE: We're doing it. We're doing it right now!

TOM: You're saying that it's not enough to just talk about or feel love, but we must move with the love and do something about it.

PAULINE: Yes. My next-door neighbor was wonderful. She didn't know a thing about herself. Very simplistic. You couldn't tell her a dirty joke because she didn't react. What a wonderful woman! She wrote a song about how "Love is the answer." So when I joined the nuclear-weapons protest at Livermore, my affinity group took that as our theme, "Love is the answer."

TOM: As you're talking, I can see the joy rising up into your eyes . . .

PAULINE: I'm boasting, if you want to put it that way. I'm really boasting about the fact that I have been able, by God's help, to believe in the supernatural, with the certainty that I don't have to be it. With that I have been able to experience love in places where you'd never expect to find it, and where, in my ordinary daily life, I don't deserve it, and it comes, I think, because I love people. They sense it and react to it.

TOM: I want to give you the opportunity now to think of or imagine something that you would like to pass down to the younger generations that has to do with this topic of love.

PAULINE: In my own personal life, I discovered that I don't, of myself, know anything. It's all been known before, so that my job is to live my life as my work. This is my work. "Of all who live I am the one by whom this work can best be done and in the right way. Then cheerful shall I greet the laboring hours. / And cheerful turn when the long shadows fall at eventide. / To play and love and rest, / because I know for me my work is best." I figure, for me, that all my work was formalized by the psychiatrist, Carl Jung, and said by Jesus in the greatest sentence in the English language. It is the first commandment of the Christian Bible: "Thou shalt love the Lord with all thy mind, and with all thy heart, and with all thy soul, (and, I would add, heart and soul are associated—even anatomically), and with all thy might." These are Jung's four functions of expressing who we are. We usually overlook the last half of the commandment that ties it all up: "Thou shalt love thy neighbor as thyself." That means you are not only entitled to think well of yourself, but it's a duty to think well of yourself. If you're doing things that to you are detestable, and you consider them evil and yourself unworthy, it doesn't matter what the world thinks about it. It's what you think. I think that I have tried; God knows I've made a mess of so much of it. Most of the disastrous things that have happened to me wouldn't have happened if I had been loving properly. But I've got it simplified now, down to the place where my job and my joy are the same because they consist in loving all my fellow men, and in fact, all life.

Postscript

August 24, 1996
Dear Abe, Elizabeth, Jens, John, Tim, and Dee—
seven elders—total strangers, but united in loving,

The more I have thought about our topic of love the bigger and more unwieldy it became. Tomorrow I go to a tea with another group of elders; I am to bring a poem or a picture that has special meaning to me. I have been bogged down between my two worlds, not realizing that one is inside the other, not conflicting. Instead of a poem, I find myself saying one phrase over and over: "God is my saviour."

I suddenly realize that saying this has become a ritual. I always repeat it each night, usually each morning, and often during the day, frequently without apparent context. It is my oath of allegiance, and my affirmation against anything problematic or negative. I say, "Thou art the Saviour," and thus find my seat, my place, and feel safe and peaceful.

I had the tremendous luck to grow up in a Christian home, and to lose my faith and go it on my own from age nineteen to age forty-five—and then to regain my knowledge that I find God to be my saviour. Meaning among other things that Jesus demonstrated immortality; I am not afraid of death. Worms become butterflies; I know of no organism whatsoever which starts butterfly and reverts to being a worm. It's simple: "Jesus loves me." And as for me and my purpose? "Jesus wants me for a sunbeam"— my experience at age five. It will be no less true at ninety-five.

What am I here for now? Same thing. God needs me to incarnate His love just as much as I need Him to help me do it. And heavy burdens and hard times are honors, not God's malicious power drive, as is the usual interpretation of the Book of Job. God depended on Job; together they gave Satan his chance and together Job again prospered. Job answered God: "Though you slay me, yet will I love thee."

I don't just love people of my class or acquaintance or family or habits. I love life. I have had carved on my tombstone: "She knew life and loved it." I sense that God is the core, the lodestar, the center: "Thou art the Saviour."

The other major focus of my recent life is: "The time is now." I have no patience with all the investments and foundations and endowments and CDs and HMOs and insurance policies—the whole schmeer of living in fantasy land. Live *now*. I want to live today's life today. That way you know I love you rather than having to take it on faith. I want time and focus and intense energy to "Live it up, Doc, now." I want to live while I'm alive and die when I'm dead.

Thou art the Saviour; the place is here; the time is now; I love you, and I work at loving myself; if I can't love me, I can't love you. I love.

PAULINE E. THOMPSON

CIRCLE OF ELDERS

A RITUAL TO READ TO EACH OTHER

If you don't know the kind of person I am
and I don't know the kind of person you are
a pattern that others made may prevail in the world
and following the wrong god home we may miss our star.

For there is many a small betrayal in the mind,
a shrug that lets the fragile sequence break
sending with shouts the horrible errors of childhood
storming out to play through the broken dike.

And as elephants parade holding each elephant's tail,
but if one wanders the circus won't find the park,
I call it cruel and maybe the root of all cruelty
to know what occurs but not recognize the fact.

And so I appeal to a voice, to something shadowy,
a remote important region in all who talk:
though we could fool each other, we should consider—
lest the parade of our mutual life get lost in the dark.

For it is important that awake people be awake,
or a breaking line may discourage them back to sleep;
the signals we give—yes or no, or maybe—
should be clear: the darkness around us is deep.

—WILLIAM STAFFORD

CIRCLE OF ELDERS

KEN: I want to thank you all for being here. This discussion represents the culmination of many months of working together. We are a statement and reflection of people bringing their energies together to put love into action. I want to honor each of you and thank you for your gifts, for coming together with us in our experiment to see if we could bring elders together to talk about love.

TOM: I, too, want to welcome you all today for this discussion about the topic of love. First, I would like to introduce each of you. On my far left, we have with us today Elizabeth Léonie Simpson; next to her is Timothy Crocker; next to Tim we have Dee Jaehrling; and to my right is Jens Hansen. Next to him, Pauline Thompson is seated. Next to Pauline is John Wurr. Finally, on my far right is Abe Levitsky. Ken and I have had a chance to meet individually with you to consider issues related to love. Today I'd like to see if we could start with the challenge of seeing if we, as a group, can look at the meaning of love and consider what message to give to the younger generations about its importance. Where do you think we should begin with the task of talking about love?

ELIZABETH: Not by speaking as a group. I think the important thing is that we speak as individuals. I even mind a little bit the "Elders on Love" title because we are not a group. We come from very different places and have had very different life experiences. I speak only for myself and I think you'll speak only for yourself, by the time you've wound your way through the pathways to this "noble" age.

TOM: As an individual, then, where do you think you might like to begin?

ELIZABETH: I think that it's very complicated to try to consider love in the abstract. One has to think of it in personal terms. To consider it as a kind of general compassion is something very different. I do not see myself, for example, ever thinking that I could love mankind as a whole or could love a stranger. The word "love" is alien to me in that context. To lump all of its meanings together is wrong because it muddies the water.

TIM: I've been on many committees, and a committee that is trying to describe love will be like the committee that is supposed to describe a horse and comes up with a camel. Asking a committee to reach a consensus is asking us to reach the lowest common denominator. It would probably obscure the function of each of us in the process. I doubt we are a consensus.

JENS: Having evolved into complete atheism at age seventy-two, I would nevertheless like to call upon Saint Francis, who said that "giving love" is the most wonderful thing, the most wonderful thing in life. Yet I feel that he was only half right—I think that giving love and receiving love have been the highlights of my life. As a group we have a combined total of five hundred years or more of living. I imagine that each of us could look back over those years and be able to describe a time or times in our lives when being alive was like magic, because we were in love and we were receiving love.

TOM: Reflecting on your life, what comes to mind when you look back on experiences of love?

JENS: Well, if I look back, it's the love I received from my parents and gave to my parents, and continue to give to my sisters and my children and my grandchildren. I agree with you, Elizabeth. I can't love humanity. I can feel sympathetic, but I think there has to be a personal connection of some kind, a reaching out to and a receiving from the persons that you love.

ELIZABETH: I have to say that I'm very fond of Shakespeare's marvelous description of Cleopatra that turns up in one of his plays, that "age cannot wither her nor custom stale her infinite variety." I can apply it to my sense of love and personal relationship with my husband. This is one of the things that makes my life so enormously rich now. But I can recall the love I felt when I was infatuated at age seventeen, in love for the first time. I thought I had to marry a young man whom I took home with me that Christmas from college. No, it's not the same at all. Love is now a very different experience, much more profound and more enduring and rich, richer than those young, mad passions, as lovely as they were at the time.

JENS: I'm glad you added that last part.

JOHN: Well, I think I'll have to disagree a little here, because loving a person is a very satisfying and exciting thing. I was thinking of the world's problems, because we're in an election year. I received some literature from a far-right organization that I won't name, people who are advocating that everybody should satisfy their own personal desires. This is not what we need, I thought. It's not satisfying our own desires, it's implementing our common ideals that's important. That is what's necessary in the world today, and it doesn't have to take us away from love. But when we think of all the people on welfare and that sort of thing, hitting them with a stick is not going to do much good. There has to be love there. I'm sorry to broaden the discussion with that, but I did this because I read what Pauline had written, and the need for loving as a society has the same sense to me as personal love.

Maybe Pauline would like to say what she feels about the social necessity of love.

PAULINE: I find that my own concept of loving extends beyond the one that you two have expressed. I beat you by twenty years, and in that twenty years I have come to the idea that my loving is not satisfactory if it doesn't include the stranger and the evil-doer. It sounds so icky to people when there is talk about love. The scientist thinks, "Well come off it; it doesn't belong here." The essence of science is to get love the heck out of it. It's a variable they don't know what to do with. The bomb never would have been made if love hadn't been excluded from the people who were producing it.

I had an awful time with the definition of love. I have attended Quaker meetings for a great many years. The Quakers had a terrible time with Nixon when he was claiming to be a Quaker. Some Quakers in Washington D.C. were quoted as saying: "If I can't love Nixon, I can't love anybody." That absolutely threw me for two years; I could not deal with it. Finally, when reading in my dentist's waiting room, I ran into an article asking a bunch of Hollywood actors what they thought about love, and Dick Cavett came up with the idea that love was "wishing people well" or "wanting what's best for them." I thought, "Well, that makes it easier, because I don't know anybody else in the world whom I would wish well more than I would Nixon. [laughter].

I have managed finally to love everybody, and it's a darn good thing I do because I don't have the props that you have. But I do have a different prop than most people. I have the one that says that we were born related to God, and I have a definition of God that includes Him in my personal life. I have to personify Him. I pray to keep up the link, and I use the word "religion" in a sense that means to re-link yourself to the supernatural. God, being the whole schmeer, can't reduce Himself to human size. So the stable, everlasting, eternal, immortal God created us to tell Him what it is to be human. My idea is that I should learn to love myself. I told myself, "If I learn to love myself, then I will be able to love others."

JENS: I like that a lot. I don't think that you can expect to find love or, more especially, receive love if you don't have a sense of worth for yourself. Otherwise it will seem fake and undeserved.

ABE: There's another point which I derived from what Pauline has said. There can be a danger of getting stuck or sticky in love. Where there's genuine love there is also a capacity to feel anger in its absence, angry at injustice and phoniness and hypocrisy. I think we need that anger to fuel our love. But as far as using Brother Nixon as some sort of a litmus paper, I would agree that "If you can love him, you can love anybody."

TIM: The power of both love and hate is really the same power: They're both the power of commitment. The opposite of love is not hate, but indifference. Love and hate are really part of the same force. I am very much attracted by Abe's point that hate is a very critical and important feeling because it carries passion equal to love, and indeed has a breadth that affects how we engage ourselves in the world. But I do share with you, Pauline, the idea that to love Nixon is to put yourself to an ultimate test.

To have done so is a true achievement, and I am grateful because Nixon does need it, and I think, in some ways, has come to deserve it. I'm not quite sure that I fully agree about his rehabilitation.

But I have a feeling that without love many of us would never have become whole. To give love is as important as to receive it. To give love is to honor someone in a way that is perhaps beyond his or her rights, but it is still vital to love because it gives us the humanity that we cannot be without and still function properly in the outer world.

ELIZABETH: The problem with what you just said is that it's too all inclusive. We need separate words for this. I can't imagine loving an abstraction. I've complained about Carl Rogers; I think his eternal "unconditional, positive regard" is hooey. I think that there is no such thing as regarding anyone unconditionally—positively or negatively. When I talk about love, I want to be very clear, whether I'm talking about it in moral terms or talking about an abstraction that's separated from me as a person and a human being. Talking about it in abstract ways—as a broad concept—doesn't have meaning to me. The same thing is true with the concept of God. I don't want to think of a spirit or a force in anthropomorphic terms.

DEE: I think that part of our problem, as Elizabeth said, is finding a different word for different ways of loving, different kinds of loving. We might take the extreme example of parents who have to deal with their children out of love and respect for them, and who sometimes have to attach the adjective "tough" to love. That means doing something that may be a total opposite of what we normally believe love to be, which might, for instance, involve putting the children out of the home, or in the care of somebody else. We might think of that as a rejection, but it's not always a rejection. Sometimes it is, but sometimes it's out of the greatest love parents can show for their children, because they no longer have the skills to do what is necessary. Then, when Tim used the words "hatred" and "love" at the same time, I think of the prayer of Saint Francis when he said, "Lord, make me an instrument of your peace. Where there is hatred, let me bring love." I thought how I've heard this prayer for almost my entire life, because I was taught by the sisters of Saint Francis— and never once did I question what Saint Francis meant by love! I never questioned it. But now we are discussing all these other interpretations of what love could be and I do think it's extremely important that we do, because we love our neighbor differently from the way we love our family. If you love a stranger, that stranger is no longer a stranger. So the problem is appropriate definitions.

TOM: We shouldn't get too caught up with definitions of love. Is there something about the awareness of love that we could convey to others? Maybe it has to do with acceptance and consciousness-raising, but is there something that people can be educated about?

ELIZABETH: I don't think it has to do with acceptance. I know some clinicians would differ with me on this point very much, but it isn't a matter of simply accepting what you experience in another person or in the world as you encounter it. I don't think that is love; I think that's useful and important but not love.

TIM: I have to disagree with that. I think acceptance is the issue of love. I think that to accept is not to judge or reject. The act of acceptance is a genuine offering of one's self to receive that person. I wouldn't be unhappy at all if Saint Francis' prayer were to say, "Where there is hate, let me overcome indifference." But I think he was referring to anger and animosity when he said, "Where there is hate, let me bring love." The idea of acceptance may be something that comes out of my medical background. This idea is that one has to accept all persons in whatever condition they are. This is the act, in a way of openness, which I have often thought was love. The unconditional love of Carl Rogers, the unconditional, positive regard, is exactly that. It is an acceptance, and I don't think it's a false idea, for me at least, in my viewing of what love is.

I view acceptance as unconditional reception. If I impose conditions on my relationship with my wife, for example, it impairs my relationship with her. The fact that she is not perfect, as I am not, means that I have to love her imperfections. The fact is that she and others are not up to my expectations. My expectations, then, must not stand between me and loving. If I expect a certain kind of treatment and don't get it and, thus, do not love, then I am being conditional in my relationship to others. I don't mean to deprive you of your right to take the terms in a different way, but without acceptance, I couldn't function.

JENS: I totally agree with Elizabeth and I have to disagree with you, Tim. There are people who have been born on this earth under horribly unfortunate conditions whose behavior is totally unacceptable. There never was a time when there weren't rapists of young girls. For the last year and a half, the newspapers have been filled with stories about an individual who raped and murdered ten young girls. I find that person totally unacceptable. I can have compassion for that person growing up as a child, but it is difficult for me to extend my compassion to acts of murder or rape.

TOM: It sounds like you are talking about a barrier for you . . .

ELIZABETH: I want to respond to what was just said. Because it seems to me that love, at least in maturity, has to be earned. It isn't an abstraction; it is a response. I hope this doesn't sound terribly behavioral, but love is a response to what you see or hear or believe about other human beings. If that doesn't occur in a particular way, then you don't love.

JOHN: It is extraordinary that I get along with my wife so well, because I disagree with her entirely. Maybe you can say love has to be earned, but that's no solution to the world's problems. We must go beyond that. We're in a very primitive state, in my opinion. I know this sounds awfully condescending, but when people do these terrible things, you have to have some pity for them, but not for doing these things. Somehow you've got to find out why people do these things, and they need our love to help them out with that.

TOM: Do we have some responsibility to try and stay with these heartaches as opposed to running away or retreating into hatred?

JOHN: Absolutely.

TOM: But I don't think that's something that we're in agreement about.

JOHN: I feel strongly about this—that it's so easy to write these difficulties off. One could say, "Throw these people off welfare and then they'll put themselves right." The fact is, I don't want to get deeply political, but a lot of these people don't have the self-confidence or the ability to get jobs. This punitive sort of thing is never going to work. This is an absence of love! We've got to help these people. We are luckier than they are because we grew up in better surroundings, and surely we can see that these are just the wrong things to be doing to them.

DEE: It seems to me that we do not like or love behaviors, but we can love the person. I know that it's very hard to separate behaviors from the image and likeness of

God that we've heard about, if we've grown up in a religious atmosphere. We say God forgives, but we ourselves cannot. That's pretty harsh! It's very difficult to separate the way a person behaves from who the person really is. Are we just the sum of our behaviors? I don't know; I don't have answers; I'm asking. I am not a mother, but I have mothered many children. I have always loved the children that I taught, but there were some behaviors in children I did not want in my classroom. Of course, I couldn't just send the behaviors out, I had to send the child out. So what had to happen was that the behavior had to change. And, as John pointed out, what can we do to help people with those unlovable ways of behaving so that these individuals become more lovable?

ELIZABETH: Overall, better parenting is needed. Whether that parenting occurs in school or through step-families or foster families or institutions of other sorts, that clearly is what is needed. If there is a biological reason for depravity—a very strong word—or for wrong-doing or evil-doing or whatever kind of inability to love, perhaps then there are still some social actions that we can do. But the question is how to operationalize these actions, how to put them to work in a particular society, and I think that's where we're remiss to a large degree.

JENS: We're starting to sound like a bunch of sociologists rather than a circle of elders talking about love. There is another aspect of love which you described as compassion. I can feel compassion, but I don't have to feel love. I feel compassion for almost anybody born in this increasingly difficult world.

TOM: Is there something that a person can do to assist another to mirror an alignment of openness and love?

PAULINE: We can't teach anybody, including ourselves. This business of self-esteem is not teachable. But I feel that my life is dedicated to the composition of the kind of self-esteem that raises the self-esteem of every person that hears me. I think one of the important verses in the Bible is that you should "Do good works for men to see and glorify our Father." People may stand on a street corner in order to glorify God, or people may stand on the street corner because they like to have their egos stroked. God said, "I didn't come to save those people. I came to save sinners." All of those other people on the street corner have their rewards. Let them stand there and show off. If you have a steward who fixes the books, fire him and he'll find a job where the people around him also fix the books. They'll be very happy together and we will get along without him. I think that's God's sense of humor, not God's shuffling the problem or giving up on the guy.

I think the principal evil is that we don't recognize evil for evil. We think it's better to be tolerant. If I want good for Nixon—going back to that metaphor—I'd say, "It's not good for Nixon to get away with the things he did. It's not good for him." If we love this guy and he's been so evil, he either has to resign or be impeached. Tolerance is not loving. We never get anywhere tolerating things. If you have a wide tolerance, you're not going to get any good work out of it. The measure of tolerance should not be how much people can get away with. That's not love.

My having to tolerate my own evil-doing is a tremendous test of acceptance. It's just tremendous. I still think of the two people who died because of me and my work and what I did when I was in charge of the medical ward in Bellevue Hospital. I killed them. It's not easy to forgive that. It's not easy to say it.

ELIZABETH: Did you do that deliberately?

PAULINE: No.

ELIZABETH: Then it isn't evil.

PAULINE: Sure, it's evil. That man's just as dead. It doesn't matter to his parents and his family and him.

ELIZABETH: That isn't the point. The point is the motivation. If you didn't intend to do it, it wasn't evil.

ABE: One issue that does seem to be emerging is that love ain't simple and it ain't easy. Elizabeth is suggesting to Pauline that she distinguish between evil and misfortune. Perhaps out of stress, out of absence of total knowledge, out of limited experience, she did something which seemed to have caused the death of two people. It seems unnecessarily and unproductively harsh to refer to it as evil. It's clearly a tragedy but it's not evil.

PAULINE: That's a cop-out.

ELIZABETH: I mind very much sitting here and hearing you beat your breast, Pauline. That's not fair to you, and I don't think it's fair to the rest of the world because I do think that evil exists. But I think we should confine it to cases such as Tim has referred to, where evil is extreme and clearly expressed, when you have a murderer, a rapist of young girls or young boys or whatever. I think that some white collar crime is also evil, but not quite as evil as these other things.

TOM: Is there some responsibility that each person must take in addressing evil, thinking about evil, accepting or rejecting evil?

JENS: I think one has to be compassionate but realistic.

PAULINE: And loving.

JENS: You can be appropriately loving. But I could never have loved Hitler when he was gassing seven million Europeans because they were Jewish or non-Aryan or whatever. I'll use that as the most extreme example. Hitler was far more evil than Nixon. But I agree that one has to be compassionate. I think the beginning of love is compassion and understanding. But these of themselves don't necessarily extend to love.

PAULINE: If it doesn't extend to love, it's no good!

JENS: Perhaps not for you. We have not developed a mutual definition of love. But my definition would include the desire to be in the presence of the loved one, to offer support and encouragement during difficulty, and an extension of my heart and soul. I could do none of this in the presence of the evil we have been discussing.

PAULINE: It isn't just compassion. I'm as sorry for the guy that molested the ten kids as I am for the kids. He's no more or less evil than I.

JENS: The man who rapes and murders ten young children is no more or less evil than you?

PAULINE: Right!

JENS: That's completely unacceptable to me.

PAULINE: I had every chance and every love and every help and joy and everything that he never had any of.

JENS: But we all have brains.

PAULINE: We're here testifying to the fact that we've all been loved.

JENS: That's true. I feel compassion for him if he wasn't loved as a child, but beyond that I have no compassion for what he has become. You've touched upon one thing that I think is really important. If we are to expect people to grow up to be effective human beings, we have to teach them how to behave properly and how to raise their children in a proper home. If you've not been raised in a loving home, it's going to be very difficult for you to find love as you grow up.

PAULINE: I was lucky because I was raised in a very loving home. You say you don't believe in abstractions— I couldn't agree with you more. Knowing about love is not enough. It's important to live it. The beauty of this group is that we can disagree so fundamentally about fundamental things. But we still believe that there's some common element in all of this, in each of us. We could be torn apart by the fact that you are an atheist and I'm a Christian. But we do not hate each other. We must not hate each other. And even if you hate me, your hatred does not let me off the hook. I must love you for my own sake, not for yours.

TOM: I have noticed that when I am witness to a terrible tragedy or heartbreak it takes some time before I can come back into a loving space. Is there something we can teach people about this falling away from loving and bringing ourselves back?

PAULINE: Only as far as we are aware of ourselves.

TOM: In order to do that it's almost as if we have to face each day with a consciousness of love.

ELIZABETH: This appears to be a sociological question. If you don't have the resources—psychologically, physically, emotionally, or socially—and unless you grow up with or at least encounter somewhere early in life the ability to cope with this world, you can't be taught anything from here to high water.

TOM: Is there some hope or encouragement we can give to help people to stay present and loving and tolerant in the face of enormous heartbreak and terror and despair?

ELIZABETH: Some people find that strength in religion. Some people find it in other social resources.

Dee, you told me that you were a Franciscan nun. Many people considered that Saint Francis was really more worthy of being apotheosized than Jesus because of his concern for the natural world and the good, basic things in the world. It seems to me that if you live in an environment like that—that is, not just one that accepts you but that provides you with day-to-day basic things—you're going to be a very different person.

DEE: Love is never separated in our emotions. We have all kinds of conflicting emotions that may even seem as though they were canceling out love. When you asked your question, Tom, I thought of times when you can become so angry with someone that you have to walk away from that person. But you can say, "I love you very much, but right now you are making me so angry that I need to get away." And so you remove yourself. The words are an acknowledgment of the person. But often we are at a loss for words, and all a person sees is our anger and not the love. That's why when we don't say the words, we come back to the person we loved, because we feel there's some mending to do. But then, Elizabeth asked, Why do we do that? We have the skills to do that. How do you teach someone such skills? It goes back to helping young people. To love also means helping them to face the consequences of unacceptable behavior, and that often appears like discipline. Discipline becomes a bad word sometimes because it's like punishment. But that's an example of why love embodies so many factors. That's why it's so hard to say "love is—" because there are so many emotions that come into it. So many factors to show that we're loving.

JOHN: We've come to an interesting question: unacceptable behavior. I disagree with my wife and I totally agree with Tim. At some point we have to make the decision about what is acceptable and what is not. This is very slippery. For example, there are those today who don't think gay partnership should be recognized, and then there are people who think it's evil not to do so. It's tricky and difficult. What actually is unacceptable behavior?

ABE: What I'm noting, and this has been suggested by several people, is that we can't talk about love in and of itself. We have to see it in the broad context of the totality of a given behavior which includes such qualities as courage, wisdom, savvy, love of truth. For instance, when you say, John, that you can love your wife in spite of the fact that you find yourself so often disagreeing with her, you're talking about your love of the underlying truth that you both have a loyalty to each other—one of the factors, I'm sure, that keeps you together.

I'm reminded of the time when I was a member of an organization—I don't know if it still exists, but it was an organization to help addicts—and when the leaders of the organization got together for their decision-making and meetings, they would begin by playing with each other what they called "the game." The game is one in which every person had a turn at being in the so-called hot seat. There, one of his or her shortcomings and foibles was picked on, highlighted, and worked over so that during the course of an hour or two of playing the game, the players got out of their systems a lot of their venom, their pettiness, their angers, and their prejudices. After that they were ready to sit down and take counsel together, and, in a sense, to be wise and loving. I think there's a great deal of wisdom in that and what it points to is a kind of appreciation and love of human nature. In order to be loving, we must recognize that we have immature sides, dark sides, and petty sides. Unless we take those negative sides into account, we're going to be silly or ineffective or shallow.

TOM: You're bringing up a good point. Maybe part of being a whole person means that we're not just goodness and sweetness, but also bad, frail, and wounded.

ABE: Exactly. My teacher, Fritz Perls, called it "real," to be a "real person." An example of teaching it would be that, when an infant or small child is having a temper tantrum, one way the parent can teach that child is to be accepting. To help the child deal with that tantrum the parent tells the child in effect, "People get angry so what you're doing is not such a terrible thing. You are being a person right now. That doesn't mean that you get a medal for it, but I'm not going to say to you that you are a bad little boy or a bad little girl for being angry at me or your mother, et cetera, et cetera." That's helping a person be real.

ELIZABETH: Well, when that happened in my household, I was sent to my bedroom until I got over it. I was perfectly free to cry and to holler, but I had to do it where it wouldn't trouble others.

JOHN: I must remember that one. [laughs]

ELIZABETH: I think that Fritz Perls had some very good ideas with regard to his philosophy, but I think he carried them to extremes, to extremes that were cruel in the end, in some cases.

ABE: He was not the best example of his own philosophy, that's true.

ELIZABETH: Exactly. I think the idea of dumping, or perhaps expelling the things that are troublesome to you because other people bait you, can only work so far. For some people, the result of that might very well be a consuming distrust, not to say hatred toward those who did it to you.

ABE: It's certainly done under controlled circumstances, but not for the purpose of shedding blood for the fun of it. In a sense it is not different from the social function of Carnival where, for a short while, people are given license for certain kinds of freedom and spontaneity that aren't a part of ordinary existence, so that they can get some things out of their system.

TOM: Do we need more rituals where a person can safely manifest some of the dark aspects of their existence? It seems to me that the individual is often trying very hard, perhaps too hard, to be good and do the right thing, and all the other aspects of behavior get closeted or punished or sent to different corners of the psyche until finally things get out of hand and the shadow overtakes the person. Do we need to recognize the darker aspects of what it means to be human?

ELIZABETH: I think it's very well to recognize darker aspects and be aware of them, but I think that, if one talks about educating or socializing, what needs to be done is to enhance the other, positive side of the personality. You can recognize what is dark in yourself, and I think that I do within myself, but I think that what has made me essentially a useful human being is that good fortune has given me a chance to be aware of how to implement the more positive side, and let it grow, and to revere it in a way that puts it to use in society and in human relations.

TIM: I do agree with the idea that each of us has to know the depths of our own shadow, our evil. Without knowing that, we aren't completely self-aware. We must learn that awareness makes the knowledge of our shadow a source of compassion, because it creates for us an awareness of humanity's wholeness. For that matter, we must develop an expanded awareness of the wholeness of God, who encompasses good and bad, the whole "schmeer." And I also agree with Elizabeth that there has to be a love of the positive, the effective, the socially meaningful, and of that which is charming and delightful and beautiful, the source of our wonder and creative effort. These efforts improve consciousness. I myself do wish to cultivate that which is in some ways exacting, in some ways difficult, and in some ways requiring intense concentration and focus of effort. Discipline is a very powerful tool that each of us must have had to use, somehow, to bring ourselves to a broader perception of the beauty of life, a state in which I think we are now. We have been given, and have called upon ourselves to give to, these socially and aesthetically valuable parts of life. But instead many of us have developed that quality of perfectionism, which calls anybody who isn't with us evil or bad or slumping or neglectful. I have to be able to say that whoever is doing a bad job, of child-raising or whatever, could have been me, and I don't quite know how to help them. The person who is an ineffective child-rearer is doing something he or she can't help; they're only doing something that is the outcome of how they were raised.

ELIZABETH: I don't accept that. With all due respect, I think that's an extremely dangerous statement. No matter how you have been treated, no matter what vicissitudes you've gone through, you are still responsible for the choices you make. For anyone to say, as the defense attorneys have said in trials of some horrendous criminals, "He was abused as a child, beaten as a child, neglected, starved," is absurd. It doesn't make any difference.

JOHN: I don't know why we haven't had this argument before when I hear the things my wife says. It's extraordinary. Sure we have freedom of choice, but I grew up in an affluent, middle-class family, in which I would be able to go to college, there was money, and there was never any problem. What would have happened if I'd grown up in an inner city? I would have gone to an appalling school where it was quite impossible to get an education. I would go out into a society where nobody wanted to hire me, a) because I was the wrong color, or b) because I hadn't had any decent schooling. In these circumstances, I might look around and see the only people who are living at all well are the people who push drugs or who are prostitutes. Parents can't be blamed for this entirely. So it's quite impossible for me to accept what my wife says.

ELIZABETH: You still have to come back to the fact that there's an individual choice and there are persons growing up in those situations who will not accept the social situation in which they find themselves. This is very difficult. Society should help these people find their way out of that horrendous situation, but still it is a matter of personal responsibility.

JOHN: The first question we ask ourselves is, "How will I survive?" When I've taken care of my basic hierarchy of needs, then I shall start thinking about other people and society and making ethical choices. I don't think about such things when I'm hungry and when I can't get a job.

ELIZABETH: We're going back to sociology . . .

PAULINE: The reason this world is in this mess is that Eros is not yet awake, and Logos has painted itself into such a god-awful corner that I think we've passed the point of no return. The conversation that we're holding will probably be completed in the next age. But now we're living alternately the life of Logos and the life of the diffuse awareness of femininity. I am trying to write a book about the cross which says that so far it's been only the "Paternal Trinity" [The Father, The Son, and The Holy Ghost]. I want to raise us out of the earth with love's saying, "God help me." We have our hands raised to heaven from our place on Mother Earth; we have Michelangelo's God reaching down, and we have the human. That's where I am. My dominant Self says that I have to contain my own shadow, but that I am contained in the sheltering hand of God.

When we become full, we add love. It's the love that's missing. The most complete description of love in the English language is in the first commandment, most beautifully translated in the King James version of the Bible, which says, "Thou shalt love the Lord thy God with all thy mind, and with all thy heart, and with all thy soul, and with all thy might." Often we neglect to add the other requirement, which says, "And thy neighbor as thyself." If we can be whole persons, loving with our minds and our hearts and in the flesh, then we do become what God said He wanted us for: we incarnate this love so that we become creators, and we ourselves incarnate by loving ourselves. We aim to become teachers but what we really need to do is to become "livers." I do think the answer to the question "Is life worth living?" depends on the liver.

JENS: I agree—be an example for others.

TOM: How do you see your role as elders in terms of addressing the problems and the ills of the community?

JENS: I would like to address the magnitude of the problem. In Christ's time there were about a billion people on earth. Two thousand years later, when we were born, the earth's population was about two billion people. In the seventy or more years since then, we are approaching six billion people. Scientists are hoping the population can stabilize at eleven billion to fifteen billion in another thirty-five years. Already, just being on earth is an incredible problem given we must stay alive and support a family. It's hard, and the impending conditions are almost beyond comprehension. What we need to do is to learn how to love each other, how to be more compassionate, how to live together without war, so humanity can be saved before we annihilate ourselves. Since we've been born, over two hundred million people have been killed in wars. Maybe twice that—who knows? What's gone wrong? I see it partly as a failure to have compassion for each other, a failure to understand each other, and—as someone has said—a failure to respect each other. I feel a necessity to remain conscious of the big issue—that the earth is in big trouble—even though in the meantime I'm eating and sleeping and making love or reading the newspaper and telephoning friends.

TOM: So one thing you're trying to do is to stay conscious of the need for compassion.

JENS: A personal goal of mine every day is to feel compassionate and to help as much as I can.

ELIZABETH: I have to object because it seems to me that it's not compassion per se that's needed. The world's population is a terrible problem, and the only way it's going to be solved is if more human beings are not produced. So we have returned to the social problems, to the fact that people have to learn about birth control and be willing to use it. We have to challenge religions which prohibit their using such tools and not depend on AIDS or on famine to wipe out the population. Compassion alone won't do it.

JENS: I agree with you a hundred percent.

TOM: What do you see as your role in terms of finding some ways to stay conscious, given the heartache and tragedies?

JOHN: Elizabeth and I talk fairly often about hatred and about indifference. How many deadly sins are there today? Surely we should include indifference as one of the deadly sins. Most often, the way we escape the enormous problems of the world is to ignore them and I think we can't keep on doing that.

TOM: Is there a way of taking some of these beliefs and putting them into action?

TIM: I've been blessed with the opportunity to do this by having taken on the job of recovery through a twelve-step program, and every day having the opportunity of being with people who are struggling also to achieve this. I have learned how to accept much of what I did in the days of my affliction and to help others to do that as well. You asked if love was a power. I say there is a Power that does this, and I think it's partly the manifestation of our concern for the person who wants to recover. I'm grateful for that because of the daily interaction with people who are looking for a way of changing their lives. This involves an awareness of the potential for goodness in people who have lost hope in their own qualities and in their own goodness. Witnessing the act of recovery is seeing the effect of caring and loving, not only by the person for himself or herself but by the others for that person. A very great gift has come to me as a result of this experience, and it still goes on daily.

DEE: I like the phrase that Tim just used, "the manifestation of our concern," because it says something which has more meaning than just the word love when we're talking about somebody that we don't know. This is when we see someone has a need and we are able to help that person meet that need at any moment. Whether or not that moment becomes longer—a day, a week, a month—we are manifesting concern, and love has a spark in it. It grows. Love is contagious. As Jens described the enormity of the world condition, we may not be able to even touch that. But by manifesting concern we can touch the condition of our families, of our neighborhood, of the small nucleus in the society in which we move.

TOM: What else can we do to put these things into action?

JOHN: You asked what we could do. It's this business of being a role-model in some respects. I greatly adored my mother and I think about the things she taught me. There are things I wouldn't do now because my mother would be disappointed in me if I did them. I've tried to give my children good standards, and hope that they will love me enough to say, "My dad wouldn't like that." But that's really very limited; we shouldn't just limit this to our families. If everybody manifests concern and does something about it, society will develop.

ELIZABETH: Part of that is, as elders, is that we not confine ourselves to a safe farm or other place to retire, where we do nothing but play games behind high walls which keep out the rest of the world. In other words, we continue to the end of our lives to be involved in other people and in the social world.

JOHN: That's very true, actually.

PAULINE: I've been trying for thirty years to write my autobiography and I have discovered that I'm never going to be able to do it because the last chapter is entitled "Now." Thirty years and I can't catch up with Now. It's got away from me. But I think maybe we're leaving out the principal ingredient and worthwhileness of developing our lovingness. It's where we're overlooking the other affirmative—joy. My image is to enjoy life. Life. Just being alive. I'm excited about being alive every time I wake up in the morning. I think, "Yesterday I muffed it. I've got to get ready for today. Today is something else again." So I have a hard time getting ready for today because I had such a full yesterday. But I clear the deck with less to get done, and love is one of the fruits of the spirit. There are also joy, peace, long-suffering, and just plain fun.

In writing my autobiography, I discovered I hadn't included any of my hobbies. So the more I made a list of my hobbies, the more I discovered that living was just plain having fun. I get along with kids because they find me having fun and then they want to have the same type of fun. If you have a toy they're not doing anything with, and you play with it, the first thing you know they want it from you. You give it to them and walk away, and, five minutes later, they're through with it. It was your fun these kids were wanting; it wasn't the toy. It was the fun.

Some of the worst things that happened to me eventually provided the most fun, because that's what I was looking for in them. It turned out that I wouldn't change one single thing, no matter what it was. Because it has brought me here. That's what is meant when you say we choose. But the grace of life is that it gives me the opportunity to make all of these wonderful choices and come out with such wonderful results. You can't tell me that anybody at my age on this planet is any happier at this minute, and that's something to be able to say.

JENS: I'm extremely happy now. Maybe in twenty years I'll be happier than you are now.

PAULINE: I don't see how it's possible. [laughs]

JENS: Let's hope I'm at least as happy as you are, that would be fine.

PAULINE: Yes, that's enough. Love is the latest attribute to develop in our human structure. I don't think we're going to have love until we are conscious of it. Like Socrates in the dialogues of Plato, Jung said, "The unexamined life isn't worth living." But my version is that "The unlived life isn't worth examining." I thank God every day that I am alive to be able to thank God. I have this friend who every time she telephones, begins by saying, "Live it up Doc, live it up." I've been living it up. It's fun.

TOM: Maybe part of the teaching is that while some serious work may be ahead of us, we also need to have some fun while tackling some of the problems.

ABE: I have two reactions when I listen to you, Pauline. One is a proposed title for your book inasmuch as you find it impossible to catch up to the now. You might call your book *The First Posthumous Autobiography.*

PAULINE: I like that. Thank you.

ABE: The other thought I had as I was hearing about the love of life, the role of fun, and your feeling of gratitude to God is: Wouldn't it be nice if your gratitude were a two-way street, that He were grateful to you also?

PAULINE: I do think that. Yes, just going one way you never get anyplace.

ABE: God is grateful to you for demonstrating that not everything is in vain, not everything that He manufactured was in vain.

JENS: Life is wonderful, isn't it, Pauline. It wouldn't have occurred to me that, when I reached my seventies, I would be entering some of the happiest days of my life. Yet every morning when I wake up I'm excited and wonder what I'm going to do, with whom I'm going to talk, and with whom I'm going to interact. I think one of the nicest things in life is to be with other persons. Not just the people I'm in love with. There are many people I like, respect, and with whom I like to listen to and exchange ideas. I hope many younger people are interested in finding out what we older people are all about, what we have inside of us. As we walk down the street, we are living examples of what life can be. If you're happy, it's going to show on your face.

PAULINE: Jesus said, "I came that you might have life and have it more abundantly."

ELIZABETH: *Carpe diem!* Seize the day!

JENS: I've really enjoyed this very civil hour and a half we've had together. We've heard differing opinions, without mounting an argument instead of listening.

TOM: I feel that today has really been an experiment. We tried to talk about a subject matter that can seem very abstract. I've appreciated all of you for working hard in a group setting to try to come up with some ideas and answers to this. I want to close by thanking you all once again for your time and your efforts, your concentration and your wisdom.

DEE: Thank you, Tom. Thank you, Ken. It's been a real honor for me to meet all these people I'd never met before. Now I feel a special bond with each one of you.

Postscript

February 1, 1997
Dear Ken and Tom,

Several times in my life, I have thought, "I have lived it up and now I should write it down." Each time, it has developed that in writing it down, I had found that I had only prepared to live it up, that I had really never seen at the time where I was going. Only in retrospect can I now see larger views of where I have been.

On August 25, 1996, I met six other "elders" whom, up to that time, I knew only as names and we spent a couple of hours in a dialogue on the subject of love. I originally had expected this to be an interesting expression of my part in past events. I had no inkling that this brief encounter with strangers would lead me to entirely new vistas from which to re-explore my long, confused, diverse life. I am re-experiencing from a different vista point. It is all new and exciting. Every morning: What am I going to think today!

I no longer feel that I will ever be able to sum up my life because each sum has so unfailingly foreshadowed a larger, more beautiful, more synthesizing new future. "Let each new temple nobler than the last shut thee from heaven with a dome more vast," said Oliver Wendell Holmes.

Last Sunday I had an experience of immortality during a Quaker meeting for silent worship that I would never have had without our August 25 meeting. Before I tell this experience, I want to say that August 25 also gave me a new slant on synchronicity, a topic in which I have been interested for several years—in fact, many years. (Jung, who died in 1961, wrote on synchronicity.) I do not see synchronicity as a new phenomenon. The reason we have sychronicity as a concept is that all events do meaningfully coincide. We give meaning by recognizing it, not by creating it. By coincidence, then, I arrived at the meeting house early and on a day when there was a hymn-singing before the meeting. I was the first one there and I found myself asking for the song, "We Shall Gather at the River."

The reason I asked for this song is that I am currently crucially involved with the sad old age of a lifelong friend. She is now without old friends, like me; we have outlived them. And she is without her own mental capacity. And without any ability to maintain the lifestyle she wants. She has never had any religious conviction of any depth. She has lived a fantastically rich and experienced life—no, not experienced—that's the point. Full of experiences but not really experienced.

In thinking of her situation in relation to my own relationship to the elderly, (and I myself am almost ninety-two) I thought of my Aunt Eva, who died in 1921 after having lived ten years following a stroke, entirely physically incapacitated. All I remember her saying during those ten years was, repetitiously, "Dear God, please let me die." And I thought of my friend Angela, whom I intended to visit in her retirement home. She lived in Ventura, and my cousin and I, because of my driving problems, drove on through Ventura on a trip to Mexico, planning to stop on the way back instead. When we did, we found that Angela had died in the meanwhile. And then there was my schoolteacher friend, Emma Newland, and my first boss, May, the librarian, when I was age eleven. Both Emma and May were found dead in their homes three days after their deaths.

I want to leave these associations for a moment to say that, for years, I have also pondered the meaning of "in my name": "When two or three are gathered together in my name." I have often thought that many Quaker silences are not centered at all; each one sits in his personal center, maybe deeply centering, but not group-centered. We come—and go—in our own names. What does "in his name" mean?

Well, I had an overpowering synthesis of all of us—all of us, regardless of time or country or space or name, Angela and May and Eva and Violet and me, and those I helped die on the psychiatric wards where I was a night nurse, and the hundreds whose deaths had touched me personally in World War II, all gathered together on the shores of the river that "flows by the throne of God."

And I had another image I treasure. I see myself in high school physics lab. I had just been issued a drop of mercury for the day's study. I have not the faintest idea of what the day's lesson was supposed to instruct. I do remember vividly, as if it was this morning, how I hunched over my microscope, fascinated to see how I could scatter that drop into a thousand smaller drops spattered all over the glass, some so small that I was aware that there must be other drops smaller than I could see. And then I could reassemble my original drop ready to return it to the lab office. The same drop. The same drop.

That's what it is to be immortal. All our different names and time and egos and locales. It's not Jesus or Buddha or Confucius or Gilgamesh or Shiva. We can see how Ellis Island changed many names, but we cannot see ourselves in all these separate names brought together at the same picnic spot beside the river that flows by the river of God. We are all eternal parts of one universe and we are each one—a separate universe within it.

This was a wonderful experience. It redeems those earlier times when I left all those fellow sojourners in the relatively murky fog in which they died. We can redeem them, update them, climb out into the light ourselves, outwit death. I have gathered us, all those parts, those "past lives" of me together. We gathered by the river.

All this joy came about partly because of our "elders" talk on August 25. Basically, I can pin it down into one sentence. Elizabeth had said to me, "When you get off this breast-beating, maybe I can respond to you." I was saying that I loved everybody or, at least, I should love everybody. And when she challenged me, I wasn't sure that she wasn't right. But our companionship in love that day took me to a deeper place than I had ever been before, and I found in that deep place that I do indeed have to love everybody. (Thank God I feel under no obligation to like everyone; in fact, I find that I shouldn't like everyone.) There is no basis for action, for life, if I cannot discriminate. I may even have to change the environments of others by force and against their wishes. But I must do so in love.

But I have to love everyone. That is not to say that everyone should love everybody. It is just that I learned in following up on that day that I know now that I have to love everyone. And I do, and I feel whole. And organized. I am me, and I am more all in one piece than ever before. Peace, sisters, it's wonderful!

I wouldn't recognize a single person in the group if we met in mixed assembly. But I shall love each of them in a special, rewarded, redeemed way for as long as, well, forever. What do you mean "as long as I live"? That's only time; the spirit is eternal.

I do like the concept of the collective unconscious as being universal. And cosmological. And galactic. And all of them big, BIG words. At the same time, it is also small and personal and individual. A really wondrous idea—that in this enormous world and time and timelessness and space, there is a place for me!

This doesn't make Euclidean sense, but it makes a beautiful spiritual, artful, religious sense.

PAULINE E. THOMPSON
"I am a discrete part of all that I have met."

ABOUT THE AUTHORS

KENNETH ROBERT LAKRITZ

I WAS BORN in New Jersey in 1958, the second of three boys to Jewish parents, Marlene and Arnie. My upbringing involved exposure to many different wisdom traditions, and gave me a broad appreciation of the numerous religious, spiritual pathways. More recently, my explorations have taken me back to my religious roots, with my growing, evolving interest in Jewish mysticism and the Kabbalah.

This project with elders, which involves the need to bring the generations together in deeper dialogue, holds great meaning for me. I believe that this work will be more and more essential as our senior population grows, and as we all eventually reach Elderhood.

I live with my wife, Robin, in Sonoma, California, amidst a thriving community of very loved and loving friends. I practice psychology in Napa and Sonoma, and am a clinical psychologist, having received my doctorate in psychology from the California School of Professional Psychology at Berkeley. My interests in poetry, fiction, and nonfiction writing have continued to blossom throughout the years.

THOMAS MORRISON KNOBLAUCH

I WAS BORN in Minneapolis, Minnesota on May 4, 1951. I was the youngest of four children, with two older brothers and an older sister. I consider myself very fortunate with respect to the opportunities and advantages I have been given in my life. I grew up with a deep appreciation for the beauty of nature in my home state, and to this day carry its image in my heart.

I left Minnesota at age eighteen to attend Yale College, where I slowly and painfully began my journey of awakening at age nineteen, after the death of my mother. I graduated in 1973 with a B.A. degree in Psychology and Philosophy. Shortly after my graduation, I began what has been a life-long love affair with T'ai Chi Ch'uan, which to this day is one of the precious jewels of my soul. I enrolled in a Doctoral Program in Clinical Psychology at the California School of Professional Psychology at Berkeley, where I received my Ph.D. degree in 1984.

In July, 1983, I met Laurie Wilson at the Child and Family Center in San Francisco. I moved in with her after our first date on August 31, 1983, and we have been together ever since, our marriage taking place at her parents' home in Napa, California, on July 14, 1984. We have two wonderful sons, Nicholas, age ten, and Noah, age eight, who fill our hearts and lives with love.

I currently practice as a clinical psychologist in Napa, California, where I have worked since 1986.

NOTES

p. viii, Epigraph 1: Paulo Coelho, *By the River Piedra I Sat Down and Wept* (San Francisco: HarperCollins, 1996), p. 33.

p. viii, Epigraph 2: Mahatma Gandhi, in *The Words of Gandhi,* selected by Richard Attenborough (Newmarket, 1982).

Preface

p. xv, Epigraph: Jesus, The Gospel of Thomas, *The Hidden Sayings of Jesus*, interpretations by Harold Bloom (San Francisco: HarperSanFrancisco, 1992), saying 70, p. 53.

I. INTRODUCTION

p. 1, Epigraph: Zalman Schachter-Shalomi, and R. Miller, *From Age-ing to Sage-ing®: A Profound New Vision of Growing Older* (New York: Warner Books, 1995), p. 189.

The Courage to Ask the Question

p. 3, Epigraph: Rabbinical story quoted in C. G. Jung, *Memories, Dreams, and Reflections* (New York: Vintage Books, 1965), p. 355.

1. Andrew Harvey, *The Return of the Mother* (Berkeley, Calif.: North Atlantic Books, 1995), p. 156.

2. Quoted in Harvey, *The Return of the Mother,* p. 179.

3. Story told to Kenneth Lakritz personally by Winston Valois.

4. Coleman Barks and John Moyne, *Open Secret: Versions of Rumi* (Brattleboro, Vt.: Threshold Books, 1984), p. 15.

5. T. S. Eliot, "Little Gidding," lines 239–242, in *The Complete Poems and Plays* (New York: Harcourt Brace, 1952), p. 145.

Re-Awakening Elderhood

p. 13, Epigraph: Rumi, in Coleman Barks and John Moyne, *Open Secret: Versions of Rumi* (Brattleboro, Vt.: Threshold Books, 1984), p. 7.

1. Robert Lawlor, *Voices of the First Day: Awakening in the Aboriginal Dreamtime* (Rochester, Vt.: Inner Traditions, 1991), p. 8.

2. *The Napa Sentinel,* December 4, 1990.

3. Murray Stein, *In Midlife: A Jungian Perspective* (Dallas: Spring Publications, 1983), p. 3.

4. *Betwixt and Between: Patterns of Masculine and Feminine Initiation,* edited by L. C. Mahdi, S. Foster, and M. Little (La Salle, Ill.: Open Court, 1987), p. x.

5. A. Stevens, *Archetypes: A Natural History of the Self* (New York: William Morrow, 1982), p. 159.

6. From "Senex and Puer: An Aspect of the Historical and Psychological Present," in *Puer Papers,* edited by James Hillman (Dallas: Spring Publications, 1979), pp. 4–5.

7. Zalman Schachter-Shalomi and R. S. Miller, *From Age-ing to Sage-ing®: A Profound New Vision of Growing Older* (New York: Warner Books, 1995), p. 5.

8. Ibid, p. 76.

9. R. Fleming, *The Wisdom of the Elders* (New York: Random House, 1996), p. 193.

10. Ram Dass and Paul Gorman, *How Can I Help?* (New York: Alfred A. Knopf, 1987), p. 17.

11. Arthur Amiotte, "The Call to Remember," in PARABOLA Magazine, Vol. XVII, No. 3, Fall 1992, p. 32.

12. C. A. Bates, *Tales of the Elders: A Memory Book of Men and Women Who Came to America as Immigrants, 1900–1930,* from the chapter, "Life in Little Italy: A Shoe Boy Survives" (Chicago: Follett Publishing, 1977), p. 65.

13. Richard Simon, interview with Robert Bly in *The Family Therapy Networker,* September/October, 1996, p. 58.

II. ELDERS ON LOVE

p. 31, Epigraph: Kahlil Gibran, *The Prophet* (New York: Alfred A. Knopf, 1981), p. 11–12.

Timothy Crocker

p. 33, Epigraph 1: Thomas Merton, *The Thomas Merton Reader* (New York: Image Books, 1996), p. 314.

p. 33, Epigraph 2: Paulo Coelho, *By the River Piedra I Sat Down and Wept* (San Francisco: HarperSanFrancisco, 1996), p. x.

Dee Jaehrling

p. 59, Epigraph: Prayer of Saint Francis of Assisi.

Jens Hansen

p. 85, Epigraph: Johann Wolfgang von Goethe, "The Holy Longing," translated by Robert Bly, in *The Rag and Bone Shop of the Heart,* edited by R. Bly, J. Hillman, and Michael Meade (New York: HarperCollins, 1992), p. 382. (Also in *News of the Universe.* Copyright 1981 by Robert Bly.)

Elizabeth Léonie Simpson & John Wurr

p. 109, Epigraph: Kahlil Gibran, *The Prophet* (New York: Alfred A. Knopf, 1981), p. 15–16.

Abraham Levitsky

p. 143, Epigraph: Rumi, in Andrew Harvey, *Light upon Light: Inspirations from Rumi* (Berkeley, Calif.: North Atlantic Books, 1996), p. 14.

Pauline E. Thompson

p. 167, Epigraph 1: Paul, I Corinthians, chapter 13, The Holy Bible, King James version.

p.176, Epigraph 2: Simone Weil, *Gravity and Grace* (Lincoln, Nebr.: University of Nebraska Press, 1997), p. 111.

Circle of Elders

p. 190, Epigraph: William Stafford, "A Ritual to Read to Each Other," in *The Darkness Around Us Is Deep,* edited by Robert Bly (New York: HarperCollins, 1993), p. 135.

Final Epigraph

p. 238, *I Asked for Wonder: A Spiritual Anthology,* edited by Samuel H. Dresner (New York: Crossroad, 1993), p. 63.

BIBLIOGRAPHY

Amiotte, Arthur. "The Call to Remember." In PARABOLA, Vol. XVII, No. 3, Fall 1992.

Attenborough, Richard, ed. *The Words of Gandhi*. Newmarket, 1982.

Barks, Coleman, and John Moyne. *Open Secret: Versions of Rumi*. Brattleboro, Vt.: Threshold Books, 1984.

Bates, C. A. *Tales of the Elders: A Memory Book of Men and Women Who Came to America as Immigrants, 1900–1930*. Chicago: Follett Publishing, 1977.

Bly, Robert, ed. *The Darkness Around Us Is Deep*. New York: HarperCollins, 1993.

Bly, Robert, J. Hillman, and Michael Meade, eds, *The Rag and Bone Shop of the Heart*. New York: HarperCollins, 1992.

Coelho, Paulo. *By the River Piedra I Sat Down and Wept*. San Francisco: HarperSanFrancisco, 1996.

Dass, Ram and Paul Gorman. *How Can I Help?* New York: Alfred A. Knopf, 1987.

Eliot, T. S. *The Complete Poems and Plays*. New York: Harcourt Brace, 1952.

Fleming, R. *The Wisdom of the Elders*. New York: Random House, 1996.

Frankl, Viktor. *Man's Search for Meaning,* 3rd ed. New York: Simon & Schuster/Touchstone, 1984.

Gibran, Kahlil. *The Prophet*. New York: Alfred A. Knopf, 1981.

Harvey, Andrew. *Light upon Light: Inspirations from Rumi*. Berkeley, Calif.: North Atlantic Books, 1996.

Harvey, Andrew. *The Return of the Mother*. Berkeley, Calif: North Atlantic Books, 1995.

Hillman, James, ed. *Puer Papers*. Dallas: Spring Publications, 1979.

Jung, C. G. *Memories, Dreams, and Reflections.* New York: Vintage Books, 1965.

Kramer, J. and D. Alstad. *The Guru Papers: Masks of Authoritarian Power.* Berkeley, Calif.: North Atlantic Books, 1993.

Lawlor, Robert. *Voices of the First Day: Awakening in the Aboriginal Dreamtime.* Rochester, Vt.: Inner Traditions, 1991.

Mahdi, L. C., S. Foster, and M. Little, eds. *Betwixt and Between: Patterns of Masculine and Feminine Initiation.* La Salle, Ill.: Open Court, 1987.

Merton, Thomas. *The Thomas Merton Reader.* New York: Image Books, 1996.

The Napa Sentinel, December 4, 1990.

Schacter-Shalomi, Zalman and R. Miller. *From Age-ing to Sage-ing®: A Profound New Vision of Growing Older.* New York: Warner Books, 1995.

Simon, Richard. "Whatever Happened to Adulthood?" Interview with Robert Bly in *Family Therapy Networker,* September/October, 1996.

Stein, Murray. *In Midlife: A Jungian Perspective.* Dallas: Spring Publications, 1983.

Stevens, A. *Archetypes: A Natural History of the Self.* New York: William Morrow, 1982.

Weil, Simone. *Gravity and Grace.* Lincoln. Nebr.: University of Nebraska Press, 1997.

ACKNOWLEDGMENTS

IT SEEMS only fitting that we begin by acknowledging our wives, Laurie and Robin, who had to wait patiently as we worked our way through the various stages of the project. Thank you, ladies. We had to divert enormous energy into making this book possible, and we appreciate you all the more for giving us the time for this undertaking. We could not have proceeded without your love and support.

We would like to thank our dear friends Frank Varela, Winston Valois, and Greg Matsumoto, who were each instrumental in supporting us over the past several years. We owe a deep sense of gratitude for their fellowship, which served as fertile grounds for the eventual development of this project.

We wish to thank our parents and family elders for their continued love, encouragement, and faith in our abilities to manifest our dreams.

To Ron Hatten, we extend our appreciation for serving as our videographer. His technical expertise and studio preparation were critical in the filming our "magnificent seven."

To Donna Bakker, we thank you profusely for doing the tedious and thorough task of transcribing the audio recordings for our manuscript.

We thank Diana Schmidt for introducing Pauline Thompson to us. She found us an elder who served and inspired us all in her recollection of her long life.

We want to extend our deep thankfulness to our publisher, Joseph Kulin, who has, from the beginning, shown appreciation and respect for our vision and our attempts to explore and articulate the subtle nature of love. We have also been very grateful to and impressed by PARABOLA for the reverence and integrity they have shown in both their personal and business interactions with us. They are a model for publishers desiring to pursue a balance between economic gain and the dissemination of books that are of special value to the public they serve.

We want to thank our copyeditor, June Fritchman, who has shown remarkable insight in her efforts to strengthen and bring clearer focus to the book. We feel that the offering of her vision and clarity provides an added, yet silent, voice that speaks subtly through all of the dialogues and commentaries of our work.

We are deeply indebted to Reb Zalman Schachter-Shalomi for his boundless generosity and for his affirmation of and belief in our work. His contribution to the book is an offering of great meaning to us. We are very thankful to you, Reb Zalman.

We most of all wish to acknowledge the seven elders who agreed to participate in our discussions. It was remarkable to us that they managed to endure the inevitable constraints of sitting under hot studio lights and requests to film particular sequences again and again. Their commitment to the entire project, from start to finish, was an inspiration to us all.

Finally, we could not have completed the writing of the book itself without the valuable editing skills of several readers we recruited for the task. In particular, Elizabeth Simpson, Jens Hansen, Dee Jaehrling, and Pauline Thompson deserve special acknowledgment for their thorough reading of the manuscript and their confidence in what has proved to be a very ambitious and meaningful undertaking.

RESOURCES

Spiritual Eldering® Institute (SEI)
7318 Germantown Avenue
Philadelphia, PA 19119
(215) 257-9308 FAX (215) 247-9703
Toll-free Information (888) ELD-RING
www.SpiritualEldering.org
SprtlElder@aol.com

The SEI affirms the importance of the elder years, and empowers individuals to harvest their life's wisdom and create legacies for future generations. We offer workshops, a Leaders' Training Program, books, tapes, and a newsletter providing information and networking. Founded by Rabbi Zalman Schachter-Shalomi.

• • •

Throughout our project, we have sought to engage our immediate community of elders in dialogue. We also seek a response from the larger community.

We are interested in hearing from the younger and elder generations about:

- Your wisdom and views on love with regard to life-meaning, community, and relationships, as well as larger political and world issues.

- Your personal stories of love and your development into a consciousness of love.

- Your offerings and guidance to younger generations regarding issues you feel might be of importance.

- For younger persons, we are interested in your views regarding the role of elders in your life.

- Finally, your reactions and comments with regard to the material in the book, *Elders on Love*.

EPIGRAM

"What message have you for young people?"
asked Carl Stern of NBC in concluding a television
interview with Rabbi Abraham Joshua Heschel
shortly before his death.

Rabbi Heschel replied: "Let them remember that
there is a meaning beyond absurdity. Let them be sure
that every deed counts, that every word has power,
and that we all can do our share to redeem the world
in spite of all absurdities and all frustrations
and all disappointments.

"And, above all, [let them] remember . . . to build
a life as if it were a work of art."